Endorsements

This is brilliant, amazingly concise yet incredibly detailed. It gives the facts but goes beyond – it teaches. John has successfully gathered hundreds of images that are easily assimilated by the reader. *Annette Miller - Missionary to India.*

John's passion for the Word of God has culminated in a commentary that is rich in understanding that will inspire the reader to apply the unique insights to their lives. *Alan Matson – Pastor.*

John relates his wealth of insight in the Bible and natural science to the reader in easily understood terms that are compact, dense and reader-friendly. I will turn to this valuable tool frequently. *Tony Hollick – Educator.*

For always selflessly dispensed wisdom and warmth and listening with under-standing. You've encouraged and guided with patience and care, and given so much of yourself. Its in salutation of your being a reformer and builder not only of (our company) but also of our character that we as students declare you as the greatest teacher, for in your footsteps we shall follow with pride. *Staff of Company in India on departing as Managing Director.*

A Layman's Commentary

Volume 1

Book
of the
Law

**Genesis, Exodus, Leviticus,
Numbers and Deuteronomy**

John Devine M Eng Sc

BALBOA.
PRESS

A DIVISION OF HAY HOUSE

Balboa Press books may be ordered through booksellers or by contacting:

Balboa Press
A Division of Hay House
1663 Liberty Drive
Bloomington, IN 47403
www.balboapress.com.au
1-(877) 407-4847

ISBN: 978-1-4525-1177-1 (sc)
ISBN: 978-1-4525-1183-2 (e)

Printed in the United States of America

Balboa Press rev. date: 11/7/2013

Books of the Bible

Introduction - The Bible is unique - it is the oldest consistent record of God's involvement with mankind. Despite its longevity with 66 Books and some forty authors there is a unified theme throughout -
• The Bible is the self-revelation of God - his character and nature
• The Bible explains the reason for the creation of the universe, the earth and mankind - to enter into a relationship with God for eternity
• The Bible is a record of God's dealings with mankind from the beginning to the fulfillment of his plan of salvation in the coming of the Lord Jesus Christ and the spread of that message to the world.
The Bible was inspired by God – *men spoke from God as they were carried along by the Holy Spirit 2Pet 1:21*; 2Tim 3:16.

The Bible consists of two parts -
THE OLD TESTAMENT is the first great revelation of God. There are many truths about the character and purpose of God that we would not know without it. Testament means covenant - between God and man. We learn about God's relationship with people and ultimately through Abraham and his descendents, the children of Israel. The prophets foretold of one who would come, the Messiah, to establish the perfect rule.
Authors - There are 39 Books subdivided from the original 24 Books written in Hebrew over 1,500 years with more than thirty authors.
Period - From the beginning of recorded history to the birth of Jesus – over some 4,000 years.
Theme - God created all things for the purpose of relationship with mankind. He chose a people through Abraham, a man of faith to reveal himself to the world. He established a standard of life for the good of all mankind.
THE NEW TESTAMENT is the fulfillment of the expectations of the Old Testament with the coming of the Lord Jesus Christ the Messiah. Through his life, death and resurrection he removed the offence of sin to God and made it possible for those who believe in him to have eternal life.
The Old Testament is incomplete without the New Testament as the people were looking forward to fulfillment. The New requires the Old which provides explanation and meaning.

Authors - There are 27 Books written in Greek over 60 years by eight contemporary authors most of whom were eyewitnesses to the events.
Period - From the birth of Jesus to the spread of the Gospel into Europe.
Theme - God so loved the world he gave his only begotten Son that whoever believes in him shall not perish but have eternal life Jn 3:16. The plan will be complete with the return of Jesus to establish his eternal kingdom.

There are several ways of understanding the chronologies in the Bible. The durations and dates presented are to allow an appreciation of the timelines and the sequence of events.

CONTENTS

Book of the Law

The first five Books of the Bible or Pentateuch (five books) including Genesis make up the Book of the Law Deu 31:26. Law 'torah' means 'teaching' or 'instruction'. They bring together the basic understanding of the Creation and the beginning of God's relationship with mankind as it developed through one man, Abraham and his descendants who became the nation of Israel. They are as relevant today as then, in revealing God's purposes, nature and character.

They are also called the Books of Moses who compiled them from early verbal records and was instrumental in leading the people through the period of the latter four Books.

Genesis – 'beginnings'

Introduction – Genesis is revelation – God revealing his Person and his plan for creation and mankind. It describes the beginning of all things in terms that have been understood by people of all ages.

Genesis is not intended as a scientific text of the 21st century. However it describes the creation in a way that could not have been conceived by the human mind at the time it was received (pre 2000 BC) if it were not for the fact that it was revealed (compare it with other ancient writings!). Furthermore, as a basic description it fits within the framework of our knowledge today. It speaks in terms that all people can understand.

The focus is not on the scientific detail of Genesis but on the existence and purpose of God. To acknowledge God brings understanding to the Book and meaning to existence. To deny God is to produce criticism and rejection. Creation by God alone is essentially a primary matter of faith Heb 11:3.

Science cannot provide answers to the 'how' and 'why' of existence. However Genesis provides the meaning and purpose of all things.

It is also a record of people of faith – Able, Enoch, Noah, Abraham, Isaac, Jacob, Joseph – from the earliest of times Heb 11:1-40.

Genesis is not a comprehensive history of mankind. The narrative has been reduced to the basic facts needed to present the purpose of creation in a way that can be understood by people of all intellects. Yet the Bible is the oldest integrated record of the history of mankind on earth – from around 4000 BC to AD 100. It also provides the means of redemption and eternal life.

Author – The various records that made up the original accounts would have been mainly verbal until compiled by Moses who, being trained in Egypt as a prince had the skills of writing and record keeping Deu 31:24.

Period – The age of creation is not stated. A figure of 4000 BC for the appearance of Adam refers to the chronological record of the events in the Bible and is not comprehensive (ref p 95).

The purpose of the record was to present God's reason and plan for the creation. The time of Abraham's birth was around 1951 BC and the death of Joseph around 1590 BC.

Location - The Bible history began in Mesopotamia the birthplace of civilization and took place in the Fertile Crescent which stretches from Ur of the Chaldeans between the Tigris and Euphrates Rivers through

Canaan to the Nile River. Canaan was the Promised Land. It connected the great empires of Egypt, Assyria, Babylon and Persia and would be dominated by Greece and Rome.

Theme – The Beginnings of God's Relationship with Mankind
• **Beginning of the Universe** – The eternal God created all things physical out of nothing – 1:1-25
• **Beginning of Mankind** – Adam and Eve were created with specific purpose as representatives of mankind in the Garden of Eden – 1:26 to 2:25
• **Beginning of Sin** – Separation of Mankind from the intimate Presence of God because they fell short of the standard required – 3:1-24
• **Beginning of Empire** - The consequences of sin and the development of civilization – 4:1 to 5:32
• **Beginning of Judgment** – Increase of evil and the Flood - 6:1 to 9:29
• **Beginning of the Chosen People** - The call of Abraham and the Covenant Promise based on faith – 10:1 to 50:26.

The great theme of Genesis and the whole Bible is that the Sovereign Creator God chooses to enter into covenant relationship with mankind, an experience that is available today through faith in Jesus Christ 1Jn 5:11,12.

SUMMARY
God Was in the Beginning 1:1
Creation of All Things 1:2-31
The Focus on Mankind 2:1-25
The Fall of Man 3:1 to 5:32
The Flood 6:1 to 11:32
The Call of Abraham 12:1 to 14:24
The Covenant with God 15:1 to 21:34
Abraham's Greatest Test 22:1 to 28:22
Twelve Tribes of the Nation of Israel 29:1 to 36:43
Joseph, His Dreams and Trials 37:1 to 41:57
The People of Israel in Egypt 42:1 to 50:26
An Example of a Great Leader (ref p35)

GOD WAS IN THE BEGINNING

1:1 In the beginning God The Bible begins with the fact that God exists - before all things. He is Eternal, Spirit, the Procuring Cause, the Source of all things. From him all things proceeded Rev 4:8,11.

Eternal – that which has always existed - without beginning and end Ps 90:2; Is 40:28; 44:24; 57:15; Rom 1:20; 1Tim 1:17; 6:15,16. In a finite universe – beyond is the One *'who was, and is, and is to come' Rev 4:8* – the only Absolute.

• *God* - **Elohim** *(*Hebrew *El* – strong*; Elohim* – majesty, plural) – 'He who is in the highest degree to be reverenced'. The name implies Creator, Provider and Supreme Ruler 2:4-6 - unique to the Hebrew people - as apart from the man-made gods (els) and idols of the world. The plural nature of the word prefigures the Trinity 1:26; 3:22.

• *the beginning* – of the universe, heavens, earth, nature, creatures, mankind, fellowship, sin, salvation, judgment, God's chosen people - of all things. Science recognizes a beginning of space, time, matter, all things physical from an instantaneous burst of total energy Ps 33:6,9. The source & nature of energy is not understood.

CREATION OF ALL THINGS

1:2 the Earth was formless and empty – darkness - no visible light, no matter - only energy – the quantum vacuum.

The Spirit of God – hovered, brooded, intimately involved – the executive manager - we should expect that the Spirit be active in the creation 6:3; Jn 4:24; Col 1:16.

Waters – the essential and fundamental requirement for life.

1:3-4 God said – the source of the energy from which all matter and force originated – the cosmological dilemma for which science has no answer! *By faith we understand that the universe was formed at God's command - what is seen was not made out of what was visible Heb 11:3;* Job 38:33; Jer 33:25. The Bible says God created matter from that which could not be seen – ex nihilo, out of nothing. That matter could be formed from energy was unknown to science till 1905 with the discovery of $E = mc^2$.

By God's Word the heavens existed and the earth was formed - the present heavens and earth are reserved for judgment 2Pet 3:5-7.

Let there be light – light (photons, packets of energy) separated from matter – the matter dominated era. From this time there was light and elements were freed to form galaxies, stars and earth Job 38:19;

Is 45:7; Rev 21:23,24.

1:5 evening and morning – the first day – a period in terms that people of all generations can appreciate - *for a thousand years in your sight are like a day Ps 90:4.*

1:6-8 an expanse (sky) with waters above and below – water above representing atmosphere, water below representing the seas which provide the conditions for life Job 38:8-11; Is 40:12,13; 2Pet 3:5,6 - the second day.

1:9,10 sea and land - the evaporative cycle, vital for life – but unknown till the 16th century - *who calls for the waters of the sea and pours them out over the face of the land Amos 5:8.*

1:11-13 vegetation - **after their various kinds** – not progressive evolution of inanimate elements without purpose or direction, but by the will of God Rev 4:11 – the third day.

1:14-19 the heavens – the stars, sun and moon - he set them in place Ps 148:6 - the fourth day. Earth is the focus of the narrative – attention to the heavens followed. How would early mankind at the time of recording (before 2000 BC) have understood the cosmology of the last four centuries?

1:20-25 Creatures of the sea and air – fish, birds; of the land – animals, all after their kind – the fifth and sixth day.
And God saw that it was good – all that He had created v25.

1:26 Let us make man The plural reflects Trinity, God who is three in one – Father, Son and Holy Spirit 2Cor 13:14. The act of creation involved the 'Godhead' - *by him* (the Son) *all things were created Col 1:15-17.*

1:26 Let us make man in our image Mankind is the pinnacle of God's creation - a unique moral being with intellect – the image of God. Everyone has a sense of fairness, what is good and what is bad both for others and ourselves Eph 4:24; Col 3:10. Man also has the ability to choose. This image implies privilege, responsibility and accountability which had to be tested - *men will have to give account on the day of judgment for every careless word they have spoken Mt 12:36*; Rom 14:12. Man also has cognitive, analytical ability to understand the surroundings and the universe. The most incomprehensible aspect of the creation is that it is comprehensible to the creature Rom 1:18-20.

The path from atom (innate) to intellect (life) has not been identified. Human physical limitation causes many to think of God as made in the 'image of man' – a god they may choose to reject! To understand by revelation that God is eternal Spirit, not confined by the physical universe or human emotions liberates the soul.

1:27 So God created man The separation of the act from the decision shows the importance of mankind to God Is 43:7. There was purpose in this act - not the result of a countless series of random chance miniscule changes destined for oblivion - further revelation of the unique nature of God.

Male and female he created them - this shows God's intention from the beginning for a purpose, relationship and procreation - for a lifetime of commitment 2:18-25 - as confirmed by Jesus Mk 10:6-9.

1:28-30 God blessed them The intention for mankind was for good - to fill, subdue and rule. Creatures were originally vegetarian.

1:31 God saw all that he had made and it was very good –
* up to the creation of mankind everything was 'good' v25
* the appearance of man caused creation to be 'very good' v31 - the sixth day.

The purpose of the Bible is to reveal the nature of God and his relationship with mankind. We have the laws uncovered by natural science, the geological & biological records which reveal stages in the creation process consistent with the early Bible account. The explanation of Genesis is understandable by people of all generations – except by those who choose to deny it. The issue is not whether a 4,000 year old revelation from God is refuted by 21st century scientific discovery but rather if man was created by a benevolent Being with opportunity to share eternity or did life and intellect occur by chance from a single organic particle (quark) through countless changes without purpose or reason and with no destiny. This is a test of faith which each one must address.

There are many polytheistic mythological creation epics from Sumer, Babylon, Egypt, Greece, in fact from most cultures - some date from before 2000 BC. None compare with the Bible revelation of an eternal personal monotheistic Being who created mankind with the offer of eternal destiny.

THE FOCUS ON MANKIND

2:1-3 In all their vast array The whole universe is the work of God - so large, diverse, magnificent and unknowable in order to reflect his glory Ps 19:1-4.

The Seventh (Sabbath) Day is set aside for the benefit of man – recreation of the mind and body is an important principle and also time for the spirit to refocus on God v3; Ex 20:8-11.

The Godhead continued with the work of maintaining the universe without whose conscious attention it would revert into nothing out of which it was created - *in Him all things hold together Col 1:17*. This was confirmed by Jesus Jn 5:17; 2Pet 3:7.

Four fundamental energy forces hold all physical matter together – their source is unknown.

Some claim there is no room for God to intervene in the laws of nature. We live and move and have our being within the same laws from which we may wish to exclude God – yet would not see ourselves as being without a degree of freedom to move within those laws. The sustenance of the universe and the life of the believer by God is not to disrupt the physical laws but to bring meaning and purpose to existence.

2:4-25 Adam and Eve This section is not an alternative account but a summary – it proceeds from the general description of the creation to the specific purpose of God in the creation of mankind.

2:4 The LORD God – (Hebrew **Yahweh Elohim**) v4. The first use of this name **YHWH**, the Tetragrammaton, used some 7,000 times in the Old Testament. It refers to the special covenant name of God and his unique relationship with mankind, especially in redemption – written as **LORD**. The four consonants were not spoken by Jewish people out of reverence (Lord Hebrew *Adonai* 18:27 was read instead). YHWH was combined with the vowels of Lord to give the form 'YaHWeH' (English *Jehovah*) - from 1518.

The two words LORD God (Yahweh Elohim) are used to describe communion in the Garden and the Fall 2:1 to 3:24. The meaning of the name was more fully revealed to Moses at the burning bush Ex 3:14. The nature of God would not have been known without his progressive self-revelation 14:21-24 (ref p41).

2:7 The LORD (YHWH) God (Elohim) formed man - the unique nature of mankind specifically for relationship is again emphasized Ps 139:13-16.

• *from dust* – this fact would have been disputed until 1930's when it was discovered that the atoms that make up all matter including humans were created in the first three minutes of creation – we consist of stardust - along with all other physical matter in the universe 3:19.

• *breathed into him* – man became a living being. We differ from other creatures because we have God's image as well as the breath of God.

Each breath we take is given by the conscious attention of the Creator – *man who has but a breath in his nostrils Is 2:22*; Ps 104:29. The greatest offence by the created being against the Creator is denial.

God's Covenant with Man

2:8-17 **The First Covenant** Genesis reveals that the universe was created so that man may have a relationship with God. It was God's initiative to create and to provide the offer of a covenant - an agreement in which God freely provides his blessing and man acknowledges the requirements. God was to make a number of covenants including with -

Adam - life, favor and relationship in return for commitment 2:16,17

Mankind - to send a Redeemer to remove the offense of sin 3:15

Noah - never again to flood the earth 6:18-21; 9:11

Abraham - to bless all nations through him by faith 17:4,19; 22:18

Israel - to be God's chosen people to reach the nations Ex 34:10 and

David - to provide the Messiah King through his line 2Sam 7:16.

The New Covenant Finally God made a covenant on behalf of those who put faith in his Son Jesus Christ - an unconditional agreement that would bring eternal life, thus fulfilling God's plan for the creation Mt 26:26-28. A garden was specially provided in Eden v8.

The tree of life and the tree of the knowledge of good and evil – however one views these two trees it is clear that mankind was created with innocence and eternal perspective. Both options involve personal choice v9.

The four rivers suggest a location in northern Iraq v10.

The Task - man was required to care for the Garden v15.

Promise of Covenant – man had unrestricted access to God v6.

The Only Condition – *you must not eat*. It was God's purpose to test man, a condition to prove trust, obedience, loyalty, belief and faith v16. Faith and trust must be tested to demonstrate genuineness. In the same way we are tested by the circumstances of life to prove our belief and trust in God Jas 1:12.

The Consequence - *You will surely die* v17 Failure would mean separation and ultimately physical death. Man was provided with a choice - between good and evil, right and wrong, communion and independence, relationship and rebellion - it is the same today.

The Family Unit - foundation of society

2:18-25 **Man was created with the need for relationship** No helper suitable was found v20 – woman was created as a helpmate and coworker, complementing. *God made woman from the rib* – an allegory of relationship, intimacy, interdependence v22.

For this reason a man will - *be united to his wife* (synergy) *and they will become one flesh v24* The marriage and family relationship was instituted by God at the beginning for complementary union and procreation 1:27,28. This institution has proved most effective through the generations and cultures. An understanding of and commitment to this principle is fundamental to all society and successful marriage. It is significant that failed relationships have not built on this God-ordained principle v24. The passions and desires of man do not nullify this institution.

They were naked, no shame – embarrassment, sensuality and profanity regarding sex and nakedness are related to sinful nature v25.

THE FALL OF MAN

3:1-3 More subtle than any animal As darkness is the absence of light so evil is the rejection of good - symbolized by the serpent.

Did God really say? The truth was stated, then the doubt planted – a lesson for us! The focus of the devil's attack was to cause man to doubt God and his Word – his tactic has not changed - his power limited to tempting!

We may eat The woman knew the truth. Doubt raised the desire to rationalize – another lesson for us. We must embrace the whole truth of God's Word and apply it without rationalization.

3:4 You will not die A half-truth – no immediate death but ultimate physical death and immediate spiritual separation. We must beware of half-truths and short-term gains at the expense of long-term loss.

3:5 To be like God Man's desire for independence seeks to remove God from our consideration. Many choose to exclude God from their lives ever since – *the fool says in his heart 'there is no God' Ps 14:1.*

3:6 When the woman saw – it was good, pleasing, desirable – these facts did not negate God's truth. This shows the frailty of human nature. **She took some and ate** - an act of the will.

She gave it – sin brings with it the desire to entice others.

3:7 Their eyes were opened – they saw their nakedness, they were exposed to the consequence of sin - innocence was lost. They sought for covering (leaves) – to hide from God - as many have done ever since.

3:8 God walked - in the cool of the day Anthropomorphism (attributing human form to God) is the main way we can appreciate the acts of the Eternal God who is Spirit Jn 4:23,24.

The continuing theme through the Bible is that mankind may have direct communion with God – this is the purpose of the creation and life. The relationship is broken by rebellion and denial. It is now restored by the death of Jesus for all who put their faith in him.

The Result of Sin - relationship broken

3:9 God called 'where are you?' He knew the whereabouts of Adam - he knows all things. His questions confirm the way God communicates with us today – he puts questions to our minds that we must answer, then act upon.

3:10,11 **They hid** - awareness of sin makes us hide, withdraw from God's Presence.

3:12,13 The woman you put here Blame, excuses – our response to sin – man, woman and serpent. Each was called to account and judged, as required by the spiritual principles of God.

How quickly our attitude can change.

3:14,15 **God's Promise** - *I will put enmity - he will crush your head* **The Messiah**, first foretold here, would be required to remove the penalty of sin. By God's matchless grace man's redemption would come not through deeds but through the seed of the woman Mt 1:20-21; Lk 1:31-37; Eph 2:8,9. Jesus is the seed through which the promise was fulfilled Gal 3:19,22.

3:16 Woman – while suffering is encountered in childbirth blessing comes to families that seek to obey God in submission and dependence.

3:17-19 Adam – failure brought a change in the cosmic order.

• *By the sweat of your brow you will eat your food until you return to the ground v19* The hardness and frustration of life is the result of sin - to refine man to the former condition.

The world is in a fallen state, subject to frustration Rom 8:19-22.

• *For dust you are and to dust you will return v19* Death occurred despite the assurance of the deceiver v4 - *the dust returns to the ground it came from and the spirit to God who gave it Ecc 12:7.* Man can only stare into oblivion without the revelation of God.

Original Sin This act of disobedience and independence by Adam also marked the entry of sin into human nature – original sin which taints each person from birth and from which we must be delivered 6:5. To do what we know is right is often difficult - we don't have to learn to do wrong. This is defined as – *all have sinned and fall short of the glory of God Rom 3:23* – the desire to depart from the perfect way ordained by God.

It is the condition of original sin that makes us acknowledge that 'no one is perfect'. Why should we have this notion of perfection? Because the Creator God is perfect and we are made in his image Mt 5:48.

It is only an understanding of this condition that brings us to the Savior Rom 6:23. The awareness of sinful nature is recognized in the heart of discerning people Ps 51:5; Is 64:6. It is in the crucifixion of Jesus without fault that we see the full extent of the degradation of human nature when the innocent was condemned by the guilty, the one without fault, sacrificed for the offender.

The failure of organized religion in the eyes of many does not negate the eternal truths, but serves to reinforce them.

A Second Covenant

God's promise to remove the penalty of sin by the seed of the woman v15 is unconditional and was fulfilled by Jesus. Satan's power was crushed at the cross – *Jesus disarmed the powers Col 2:15; Gal 3:14,15* – the means of restoring the relationship was established and eternal life assured.

3:20 Eve - became the mother of all the living The Bible describes mankind as proceeding from one woman. Modern anthropology now supports common ancestry of man from one stock – out of Africa.

3:21 God provided skins - instead of leaves. A suggestion of sacrifice, requiring the death of a substitute animal 'in place of' the guilty Lev 17:11; Heb 9:22.

3:22 Like one of us – this cannot be understood without the Trinity. *Knowing good and evil* - with knowledge comes responsibility.

Man was made in God's image, a moral being with intellect. The knowledge of good and evil brought the tendency to rebel against God. As a result eternal life was withheld from mankind.

3:23,24 **The Penalty of Sin** - immediate exclusion from unique fellowship with God and from eternal life - symbolized by access to *the tree of life.* The unbridled self-seeking, rapid moral deterioration and futility of mankind followed Rom 6:23. The evidence and consequence of fallen nature is evident today around the world.

God's Plan of Salvation

It was God's intention to fellowship with mankind continually - *He is not far from each one of us Acts 17:27,28.* That relationship was broken when man chose to be independent from God.

The penalty of sin is spiritual death - eternal separation from God 3:22. The offence could only be removed by the perfect sacrifice of Jesus

Christ and his death on the cross gaining eternal life for all who put their faith in him as Savior and LORD Rom 3:21-31; 1Jn 5:11,12; Rev 1:7. Those who do, know the experience of walking with God in all the circumstances of life 1Jn 1:3; Rev 2:7; 21:3.

The Evidence of Fallen Human Nature

4:1 The LORD – the covenant name Yahweh 2:4 (ref p22).

Eve's statement confirmed her ongoing trust in God.

4:2 Abel kept flocks, Cain worked the soil – both noble tasks.

4:3,4 The LORD looked with favor God chose Abel over Cain! There was a previous instruction Gen 3:21; 15:9; 26:5. Abel chose to obey God - an attitude of the heart.

Abel was the first man of faith. *By faith Abel offered God a better sacrifice – by faith he was commended as a righteous man – by faith he still speaks Heb 11:4.* A principle is introduced in the life of Abel that permeates the whole of God's relationship with man - *the just will live by faith Hab 2:4* - by believing God. We are able to stand before God because we believe he is faithful and we believe what he says. Adam did not believe - Abel did! Favor with God is based on believing God *– faith, from first to last Rom 1:17.* Cain did not act in faith - his attitude towards God was wrong - he chose convenience both in choice of offering and quality. Abel was also the first prophet for he testified to the presence of God by his obedience and acceptable offering - this was acknowledged by Jesus Lk 11:51.

4:5 **Conflict** Disobedience caused enmity between brothers as well as between God and man, which could only be removed by Jesus Eph 2:14-18.

4:6-9 **The result of disobedience** God spoke to Cain about the offering, his attitude and about the outcome of his actions v4,5,6. Wrong acts lead to disfavor, pride and envy then anger and further opportunity for sin. Cain was aware of his situation. God warned - *sin is crouching at the door, it desires to have you v7* – sin can and must be mastered. God gives each person awareness of the right response and so we are without excuse Lk 15:21-31.

Despite the warning Cain proceeded – he made a preconceived plan. He continued in sin - hate, murder, lies, unfruitful, a restless wanderer.

4:10-16 Your brother's blood cries out to me from the ground We can be sure that sin will be found out, punished and justice administered. He went from the LORD's Presence – further from fellowship. The actions of Cain demonstrate the impact of sin in human nature and the consequences.

4:17-24 **The genealogy of Cain** is briefly outlined before continuing with the line of divine appointment. The background behind Cain's wife is not relevant to the narrative. She must have been a relative – the hereditary impacts of intermarriage would not yet have been significant 5:4.

The beginnings of civilization are portrayed – city building v17, raising livestock v20, music v21, metalwork v22 - increasing conflict, violence and retribution v23,24.

4:25 A new son born Seth – 'appointed' – the divine line was continued through this appointment.

4:26 Men began to call on the name of the LORD Worship of the unique **Covenant God** was developing – as opposed to polytheism.

Genealogies - From Adam to Noah

There are many genealogies from antiquity. None are as comprehensive and continuous as the Bible – from Adam to Jesus Lk 3:23-28. There may be inconsistencies but the records are given so that we may have an appreciation of the events involved (ref p95).

5:1-20 **An overview of the essential aspects of creation** Man was created in the likeness (image) of God. The narrative then continues the divine line from Adam through Seth v3.

5:21-24 Enoch walked with God Despite the entrance of sin into the world it was possible for a person to find communion with God – *Enoch walked with God 300 years* (from an early age). His relationship was so real that God took him away rather than having to experience death v24. It was by an act of faith that Enoch pleased God - was Enoch told beforehand that he would not experience death? Heb 11:5.

The principle of faith is central – *without faith it is impossible to please God Heb 11:6.* This encounter with the living God is available to each individual who will genuinely seek him, with all their heart - it is the purpose for which we were created Jer 29:13.

Enoch's faith-walk gave him insight into the deep things of God including the Second Coming of Jesus – *the Lord is coming to judge everyone Jude 1:14-15* - reason for us to walk with the LORD.

5:25-32 Methuselah died in the year of the flood, 1656 years after the appearance of Adam. When Enoch was born no one of his lineage had died except Abel. Adam died when Enoch was 308. God took Enoch 57 years later at the age of 365 (half life span!). At the time Enoch was taken no one else of his lineage had died apart from Adam and Able (ref p96). Noah was born 69 years after Enoch was taken.

THE FLOOD – The Righteous Act of the Holy God

6:1-5 The sons of God - who live independent from God Is 1:2.

My Spirit will not contend – the days of mankind were numbered v3.

Wickedness – only evil The rapid moral deterioration which followed the fall is confirmation of original sin passed on by Adam's independence v5. This is also clearly seen in the degeneration of empires and the inability of man to govern without corruption and greed Ecc 9:3. A full understanding of the degradation of human nature did not come until the cross Jn 19:4-7.

6:6,7 For I Am grieved – the sinful acts of mankind cause pain to the Creator - who is personal and holy.

6:8 Noah found favor in the eyes of the LORD As with Enoch God found one who was faithful 5:24. It was the fact that Noah believed God about the flood and acted on what he believed that he became *heir of the righteousness that comes by faith Heb 11:7.*

6:9,10 Noah walked with God A constant theme in Genesis is that it is possible for us to walk in relationship with God despite the Fall 3:8 - *the eyes of the LORD range through the earth to strengthen those whose hearts are fully committed 2Chr 16:9.*

6:11-13 God's Judgment is not vindictive or arbitrary. There are consequences for doing good and evil. This confirms the ultimate judgment of God will come on those who continue to ignore him.

The Flood has been noted in many cultures - this supports the common nature of the event. The Bible account is by far the most complete and integrated with the overall historical record - not just as an isolated event but as an integral development in the plan of God.

6:14 Noah's Faith was Tested He lived at a time when most did not believe in God - *man's heart was only evil all the time v5,6;11-13.* He was told to build an ark - to that point there had been no rain 2:5,6. Noah was told *I will send rain for forty days and nights!* 7:4. In the midst of unbelief, rejection and uncertainty Noah believed God!

6:15-17 The dimensions of the ark – 140 metres long, 23 metres wide, 14 metres high – three decks (three sports fields!) - it has actually been built in modern times. Noah would be in the ark for over one year 7:11; 8:14.

6:18-21 **The God of Covenants** - a Covenant with Noah!

6:22 Noah did everything just as God commanded v22. Obedience to God and his Word is our side of the Covenant.

7:1-24 **Judgment on Sin** Seven of every clean animal were taken for sacrifice. For forty days the springs of the deep and floodgates of heaven were opened v11; 1:6,7. The flood remained for 150 days.

8:1-22 **God remembered Noah** This was a new start for mankind. The ark is a type of God's protection for those who acknowledge Him - the promise of a remnant from the judgment of mankind 1Thes 1:10. This was the first time rain had occurred 2:5.

Noah offered a sacrifice in thankfulness v20. Mercy is part of God's holiness v21 – *the compassionate and gracious God Ex 34:6.*

Terms of the Covenant with Noah

9:1,2 Be fruitful and increase – the promise renewed 1:28.

9:3 Everything will be food for you - God's abundant provision. Humans became eaters of meat.

9:4-6 Life is in the blood – meat with the life-blood must not be consumed Deu 12:23. Life is precious in the sight of God – we are accountable for our own life and for the lives of others. There is the power of the blood of Jesus to forgive & cleanse, to heal and to overcome evil Rev 12:11.

9:7-17 The rainbow is a reminder of God His mercy and His Presence and his unconditional Covenant not to flood the earth again.

9:18-29 Noah's final involvement brings a warning of the danger of excess and the outcome v21. Shem received the divine line - Japheth received prosperity - Ham followed the way of the world through Canaan v25-28.

The Table of Nations

10:1-32 This statement is supported by the modern scientific view of the common migration of man out of Africa.

• Japheth's descendants populated Europe and south west Asia v2-5

• descendants of Ham inhabited Babylon, others moved through Africa - Ethiopia, Egypt and Canaan v6-20. Nimrod's Babylon plays a significant role in history as the personification of independence from God and his ways and will be prominent in the end time v10; Rev 18:1-9

• descendants of Shem inhabited Arabia, central Mesopotamia and the East - Assyria, Elam and Aram. Abraham migrated from Ur of the Chaldeans v21-31. Canaan is the land to be promised to Abraham v19; 15:18-21.

Noah blessed the LORD, the God of Shem 9:26 - this was a prophetic word for from the descendants of Shem came Abraham and eventually the Messiah Jesus Christ 12:3; Rom 4:16,17; Gal 3:26-29.

Why is there not more detailed information about people in many of the Bible narratives? Detail is only provided as it reveals God's purpose and his relationship with mankind, in particular through the divine line and in regard to his plan of salvation.

Independence From God – the great sin.

11:1,2 Shinar Lower Mesopotamia, identified by archeology as the 'birthplace' of civilization - the area of modern day Babylon 10:10.

11:3,4 **Mankind's desire to reach the heavens!** The sin of self-centeredness, pride and ambition - a symbol of independence from God. The plans of mankind outside of God are forever frustrated - *the nations exhaust themselves for nothing Hab 2:13,14.* Despite the Flood and the continuing evidence of God's hand in creation, redemption and judgment the hearts of many remain hard today.

11:5-9 God came down – the LORD is continually involved in the affairs of mankind, seeking relationship and setting limits.

11:10-25 **God's plan was to populate the earth** An overview of the descendants of Shem is given in preparation for the introduction of Abraham. Eber was the first of the Hebrew people 10:21; 11:16. (ref p96).

11:26-32 **Abram, Nahor and Haran** Terah had three sons. The family was polytheistic Jos 24:2. He moved from Ur of the Chaldeans 1,000 km to Haran with Abram, Sarai and Lot. Terah died in Haran at age 205 years v32.

THE CALL OF ABRAHAM – the Father of Faith 17:5

12:1-5 **Beginning of the History of Israel** Throughout the Bible we see the call of God on the lives of people. God chose to create the universe. He chose a relationship with Adam / Able / Seth / Noah / Abraham / Isaac / Jacob / Moses / Joseph. It is always God who intervenes in the affairs of mankind to ensure his divine plan is fulfilled. With each of the people chosen there was a common principle – they were people of faith who heard the voice of God and responded. In the same way if we are to be counted among their number we must believe and act in faith. *Now faith is the substance of things hoped for, the evidence of things not seen Heb 11:1; 13.* A close relationship was to develop between Abraham and God as he learned to hear and respond - characteristic of the offer of God to all who seek it.

This understanding of the intervention of God in the affairs of mankind is denied by those who seek to exclude God from the creation on the basis of the laws of natural physics. Such denial is neither necessary nor justified. The revelation of the absolute God as omnipotent lawmaker, omniscient sustainer and omnipresent provider does not contravene physics & accords with the daily experience of the believer.

The call to Abram included seven aspects v2,3 –
- *a land I will show you* - the Promised Land 15:18-21
- *I will make you a great nation* – nation of Israel Ex 1:7; Gal 3:29
- *I will bless you* – he prospered physically and spiritually 13:5,6
- *I will make your name great* – in the kingdom of heaven! Mt 8:11
- *you will be a blessing* – we are heirs of the promise Gal 3:29
- *I will bless those who bless you and curse whoever curses you* Nu 22:12 – these promises have not been revoked Rom 11:28,29
- *all peoples on earth will be blessed through you* Rom 4:16,17.

This last promise is relevant to the New Covenant and the people of the non-Jewish nations. It shows God's concern and eternal plan for all people on earth. It was **fulfilled in the death of Jesus** - providing salvation to all who respond – it also met the promise of Gen 3:15.

The call was confirmed at least six times – 12:1; 12:7; 13:14-17; 15:1; 17:1; 22:15-18. When we respond to his leading God continually reminds, directs and encourages our faith along the way.

Based on these promises Israel lays claim to their homeland.

There are three aspects of faith Heb 11:8-13
- obedience to what God asks – *when called he obeyed and went v8*
- trust in God's provision – *he made home in a foreign country v9*
- believing what God says especially about the future - *he considered God faithful who promised v11.* Abram did not see the fulfillment of the promise regarding possession of the land.

There is no indication of how Abram came to faith in the monotheistic unique triune God - as with us the important thing is how we respond.

When did Abram receive the call? In his hometown of Ur - *I am the LORD who brought you out of Ur of the Chaldeans 15:7.* He moved on from Haran over 600 km south after a renewed call Acts 7:2-4. Abram was born in Ur when Terah was 70 years old 11:26. When Terah left Ur Abram would be at least 40 (he was married and Lot was his nephew). He was 75 when he left Haran. So he may have spent 35 years in Haran 12:5. Terah lived to 205 years - another 60 years in Haran after Abram left. (Alternatively Abraham may have been born when Terah was age 130 and remained in Haran till his father died as recorded by Stephen Acts 7:4 (ref p94)).

Whenever the call came Abram was faithful in responding to it.

12:4,5 So Abram left, as the LORD had told him Heb 11:8. God continues to speak today to those who are willing to listen and respond to his Word.

From now on the narrative follows the divine line of the chosen man of faith, Abram and his descendents. All of these were commended for their faith – not their deeds Heb 11:2; 1Pet 1:7.

The Father of Faith

12:6-9 **Dwelling in the Land of Promise - Shechem** was near the future city of Samaria in a land inhabited by Canaanites and Perizzites 13:7. Abram was to be an alien in this foreign land for the rest of his life. The promise was renewed a second time so *he built an altar v7.* From there he moved 40 km south to **Bethel**, 20 km north of the future city of Jerusalem. *Abram pitched his tent v8* – he chose to live in a tent demonstrating faith. That he built an altar and pitched his tent showed his priority before God. People were city dwellers 4:17. Abram was settled in Ur and for a time in Haran. He gave up permanent residence and became a tent dweller in a strange land waiting for the promise to be fulfilled Heb 11:9. In answering the call Abram was able to be set free from the mundane things of the world to do what otherwise would have been impossible for him to do. This is an important principle of faith – *we are not of those who shrink back and are destroyed, but of those who believe and are saved Heb 10:39.* This practice was followed by his descendents Isaac and Jacob. We also need to be ready to move. It was by faith that Abram became father of the faithful Rom 4:16.

12:8 Abram built an altar and called on the name of the LORD He had to break with the polytheistic beliefs of his own people and the inhabitants of Canaan to worship one God. He had heard the call – now he was seeking communication with God for guidance on a regular basis 4:26; 13:4.

12:9 He moved south into the **Negev**, the lowland plains 30 km south of Jerusalem near **Hebron**.

12:10-20 **Trouble in Egypt** In a time of famine Abram went down to Egypt. He made Sarai tell a half-truth to the Egyptians – this displayed a definite lack of faith. What Abram feared came to pass – fear is the absence of faith and often materializes Job 3:25. We are obliged to tell others the truth about our faith and to trust God for the outcome. God protected Sarai and the future promised seed. Abram must have spent some time in Egypt but was sent away in humiliation.

Abram and Lot Separated

13:1-18 **The Promise Renewed** Abram returned to Bethel and again put his trust in the LORD. The blessing of God was clearly on Abram as well as on Lot v5,6. Why is it that those who have much also quarrel? The LORD loves unity of the brethren Ps 133.

Abram showed fairness and humility in giving Lot the choice v8,9. Lot's choice was based on the eyes – ease, self-centeredness. Was he also drawn to the sinful cities? v10-13.

Lift up your eyes from where you are v14 The promise was given a third time - when we make the right choices there is reward v14-17. We must know and apply the promises of God as we seek to serve and lead others to Christ. The LORD tells us to lift up our eyes to see the vision he sets before us otherwise we may miss it. Abram moved again to Hebron south of Jerusalem where he built an altar v18.

14:1-17 **Abram Rescued Lot** This event highlights the conflict and insecurity of the times in the Fertile Crescent. Four Babylonian kings against five kings of the south. Lot was living in Sodom – when we are attracted to the world we easily move into it and eventually embrace its ways, then suffer the consequences Ps 1:1-6. Abram's ability to raise a successful rescue highlights his leadership skills and God's blessing.

14:18-20 **Melchizedek** His sudden appearance is unexplained. He was king of Salem and priest of God indicating that God was at work in people outside of the Bible account. Abram recognized and honored Melchizedek giving him a tenth of everything. Melchizedek had no pre-history and no further activity in the Bible – little is known about him. He was a special priest of **God Most High** without known human appointment. His name means king of righteousness and king of peace

(Salem). For these reasons he is a prefigure of Jesus who has no beginning and end, is the great High Priest, Prince of Peace and future King Heb 5:6; 7:1-18. David foretold that the Messiah would be a priest in the order of Melchizedek forever Ps 110:4.

14:18 **God Most High** – Hebrew *El Elyon* – El, a singular term for God meaning First Cause 1:1 – is usually connected with an attribute of God – like 'El Elyon' – God Most High. This name was introduced by Melchizedek who was priest of God Most High.

14:21-24 Abram could now use the compound name *LORD, God Most High, Creator of heaven and earth* – Yahweh, El Elyon v22.
The fairness of Abram shows his growing dependence on God v23.

Compound Forms of the name of God which present his character and nature - as progressively revealed in Scripture - not made in the mind of man -
• **El - God** - connected with an attribute of God 1:1; Ps 63:1
• **Elohim - God** - Creator, Provider, Supreme Ruler 1:1; Ps 121:1,2
• **Yahweh Elohim – the LORD God** - God of Covenant 2:4-6
• **Yahweh - LORD** - used at the call of Abram 12:1
• **El Elyon – God Most High, Creator of heaven and earth** - introduced by Melchizedek 14:18; Ps 83:18; Dan 5:18
• **Yahweh, El Elyon - LORD, God Most High, Creator of heaven and earth** – Abram now used this compound name 14:22
• **Adonai Yahweh - Sovereign LORD** - used in the reaffirmation of the promise to Abram acknowledging the authority and faithfulness of God 15:2
• **El Roi - God who sees** - Acknowledged by Hagar 16:13-15
• **El Shaddai - God Almighty** - revealed to Abram at 99 years old as the promise was renewed for the fifth time. He received the new name Abraham 17:1 – *is anything too hard for the LORD* 18:14
• **El Olam - the Eternal, Everlasting God** - when Abraham had received his son Isaac and was at last settled 21:33; Gen 21:33; Ps 90:1,2; Is 40:28
• **Yahweh Jireh – the LORD will Provide** 22:13,14
• **Yahweh Rapha – the LORD our Healer** Ex 15:26
• **Yahweh Nissi – the LORD my Banner** - victory over Anakites - when arms were lifted up – the banner of prayer Ex 17:8-16

- **Yahweh Maccaddeshoem – the LORD our Sanctifier** - who makes you holy Ex 31:13
- **Yahweh Shalom – the LORD our Peace** Jud 6:24; Is 26:12
- **Yahweh Raah – the LORD our Shepherd** Ps 23:1
- **Yahweh Sabaoth – LORD of Hosts (Almighty)** Is 6:1-3
- **Yahweh Tsidkenu – LORD our Righteousness** Jer 23:6; 33:16
- **Yahweh Shammah – the LORD is there (is present)** Ezk 48:35

The meaning of the name of God was more fully revealed to Moses at the burning bush Ex 3:14 (ref p41).

THE COVENANT WITH GOD

15:1-6 **Justified by Faith** Many things were not explained at the first call including the location of the land and the birth of a son. God often calls and expects us to respond in faith, with the details revealed along the way. *Do not be afraid v1* – these words are often repeated in the Bible Jos 1:9; Mt 6:25,31. Doubt entered Abram's mind about the length of time for the promise to eventuate. It is natural to question what we believe – the test is what we do about our doubt. God's promises are sure and He always expects us to move in faith! Heb 11:6. The promise was renewed (a fourth time) v4,5 – we must read the Word of God daily to be refreshed about the promises of God to us.

Abram believed God v6 The promise to Abram was unconditional based on faith. He became the **father of faith** because he dealt with his doubts and believed what God had told him. This is encouragement for us to hold to what we believe despite the circumstances. *Against all hope, Abraham in hope believed and so became the father of many nations Rom 4:18.* Abram's faith finally reached maturity and as a result he was recognized by God as righteous Rom 4:3. This is of concern for those who are so bound by physical science and evolution that they are unable to engage the spiritual realm.

It was not by his works (deeds) that he was accepted but by his faith *He did not waver through unbelief regarding the promise of God, but was strengthened in his faith and gave glory to God, being fully persuaded that God had power to do what he had promised – this is why it was credited to him as righteousness Rom 4:20-24.* These things were written for our sake 1Cor 10:11. The things we do are because of our faith – this is of importance as we embrace *the righteousness from God that is by faith from first to last Rom 1:17.*

Abram's faith was again to be sorely tested 22:1. Faith is not faith if it is not being tested Heb 11:1.

15:7-21 The Covenant Established The call from Ur was confirmed. The LORD gave Abram a sign - we are blessed when we act without proof. Prophetic instruction was given about Israel in Egypt and the return to the Promised Land v13. Abram waited all day until *the sun had set* for an answer to his request v17.

The promise now became a Covenant v18. Possession of the land was achieved through Joshua Jos 1:4. The ten nations who lived in Canaan, the 'Land of Promise' are listed v18-21; 10:15-19. They would be replaced because of their evil ways v16.

16:1-12 The Ishmaelites At this stage Abram had no children despite the promise of God. Abram was required to trust God to be faithful to his promise regardless of his age or that of his wife. It was Sarai who instigated the birth of Ishmael. She acted in common sense to bring about the promise of God. Abram was prepared to respond to this lack of faith as the promise of a child to Sarai seemed remote. One can only ponder the consequence of this action by Abram. The worldly seed always seeks to persecute and destroy God's seed – Cain against Abel / Ishmael against Isaac / Esau against Jacob / Pharaoh against Moses / the brothers against Joseph / the kings against the prophets – religious leaders and Jesus. We may bear resentment as we witness for Jesus Mt 5:11,12. God continues to work his purpose through the chosen seed Mt 5:13-16. This event was all part of developing Abram's faith - he was now age 85.

Abram's lack of decision allowed conflict between Sarai and Hagar to worsen. We must deal with problems as soon as they occur v6.

God had a plan for Hagar which required coming under authority and submission – a common character building experience v9.

16:13-15 God Who Sees - (Hebrew *El Roi)* - further revelation.

A NEW NAME – Abraham 'father of many'

17:1-27 God Almighty - Hebrew *El Shaddai* – a compound name revealing more of God's nature. God revealed himself as Almighty when Abram was 99 years old. He appeared and renewed the promise for a fifth time. We need to be reminded that God Almighty can do mighty things with and through us despite our age.

He fell face down in reverence v3, 17 - we must learn to walk before the LORD with humility, awe and worship Heb 12:28,29.

Abraham, father of many nations v5 This name was fulfilled in the spiritual realm for people of all nations who put their faith in Jesus become children of Abraham and heirs of the promise Gal 3:7,14.

The whole land of Canaan – center of the Fertile Crescent from Mesopotamia to Egypt v8; 15:18-21; Deu 7:1. The covenant was confirmed by circumcision as an outward sign v9-14. Sarai became Sarah 'princess' v15.

The promise would come through a son born to Sarah – Isaac was God's choice v16. There was still doubt that God could do the impossible v18,19 - compare Abraham's reply with that of Mary mother of the LORD Lk 1:37,38. That he laughed within himself was due to joy at the incredible nature of the promise. We must learn to accept the impossible as we walk with God Mt 17:20.

18:1-8 **The Royal Visit** The LORD appeared to Abraham as three visitors – reference to the Trinity? We must be careful how we react to strangers who may be angels in disguise 19:1. Abraham offered hospitality and kindness - so should we Heb 13:2. His hasty actions anticipated a major event. The purpose of the visit was twofold - to prepare Sarah for the promise and to punish evil.

18:9-15 **Sarah's Test of Faith** The promise of the miracle birth was confirmed for a sixth time to Abraham v10. Sarah overheard the conversation with the visitors and laughed to herself in unbelief. When questioned she denied her action in fear of those who could both promise the impossible and know her thoughts. *Is anything too hard for the LORD? v14.* She came to the realization that she also as partner must be committed to this act of faith.

Destruction of Sodom and Gomorrah

18:16-33 **The Power, Privilege and Purpose of Prayer** The LORD includes the faithful in what he plans v17. The promise is to those who teach their children to keep the way of the LORD v19 - this is our Covenant duty. God always brings about what he has promised to those he has chosen.

The outcry came to God - evil will not go unrestrained or unpunished v20. *I will go down and see v21* God sees all that takes place - good and evil. Nothing escapes without judgment. We will all have to account Rom 14:12.

The people of the city demonstrated the degradation of the independent heart in unrestrained sodomy - denounced in the Old & New Testaments Lev 18:22; 20:13; Rom 1:24-27.

The Prayer of the Righteous Abraham's heart was revealed as he pleaded for Sodom to be spared. What can we learn? God's mercy will always reach out to the penitent - the Judge of all the earth will do right! v25. We are encouraged to pray for nations, leaders, family and all saints Eph 6:18; 1Tim 2:1-3. We may plead the cause of others in intercessory prayer and be the means God uses to save them v32. God always engages in our prayers v33; Rev 8:1-5 – the prayer of a righteous man is powerful and effective Jas 5:16.

That the LORD confided in Abraham even though he knew what he would do shows that he enjoys communion with us v17,33.

19:1-11 The Sin of Sodom Opportunity was given for Lot and his family to escape and for the town-people to repent.

19:12-29 The Downfall of Lot Attachment to the city made him reluctant in the face of urgency but the LORD was merciful v18-21.

Do not look back – the requirement of repentance v17. Lot's wife suffered the consequence - swept away in the judgment v26.

19:30-38 The final state of Lot's family – recall the position of Lot when he chose the plain and the pleasures of the world 13:10. The Moabites and Ammonites would be in conflict with Israel in the Promised Land.

Abraham and Abimelech

20:1-18 Abraham moved back into the Negev, to Kadesh 100 km south of Jerusalem. Again Abraham showed lack of faith by requesting that Sarah lie. God spoke to Abimelech – God intervenes in the world to protect his plan v3. Abraham was acknowledged by God as a prophet v7. Abimelech acted responsibly towards Abraham and Sarah. Again Abraham the father of faith had to have his faith tested and developed for greater tests Heb 11:17. We can understand from this that our faith will constantly be tested that it *may be proved genuine and result in praise, glory and honor when Jesus Christ is revealed 1Pet 1:7*. Faith is made prefect through testing Heb 5:7-10.

Birth of Isaac (laughter) – Son of the Promise

21:1-8 At 100 years of age Abraham received the promised son by Sarah.

21:9-21 God's Sovereign Choice We are reminded that God is always faithful to fulfill all His promises 2Cor 1:20. Sarah's resentment towards Hagar and Ishmael remained and caused separation. God promised to make a nation of Ishmael because he was Abraham's son! v13. The selection of

Isaac, the spiritual younger son (born in Sarah's old age) over Ishmael, the eldest natural son again shows God's sovereign choice Rom 9:7,8.

The name God (Elohim) is used outside the Covenant v17.

21:22-32 Abraham made a treaty with Abimelech at Beersheba, 80 km south of Jerusalem over a disputed well. This was a time of great thanksgiving for Abraham – he now had the son of the promise and a secure location.

21:33,34 The LORD, the Eternal Everlasting God - Hebrew *El Olam* – a compound name emphasizing God's eternal Being v33. Abraham had come to realize that God is eternal and that he will always bring to completion the things he asks us to do.

ABRAHAM'S GREATEST TEST

22:1-12 When all the struggle appeared to be over – God tested Abraham! He was called to perform a heathen sacrifice on his son of the promise! We can learn much from the **father of faith** -

• Faith must be continually tested Heb 11:6 - so that you may be mature and complete, ready for anything Jas 1:2-4

• Faith is perfected through suffering - obedience is proven Heb 2:10,11

• Our greatest test may still be ahead! Heb 5:7; Mt 26:36-39

• The test may not make sense at the time Heb 11:18

• We may not have all the details at the time v1,2; Heb 11:8

• The test may be between you and God – it may not be understood by others

• God's glory is served through our testing 1Pet 1:7.

It is confirmation of Abraham's developing faith that he obeyed without delay despite the enormity of the request. He had come to the place where he held God's Word in higher esteem than his feelings or reason. We may not understand how to reconcile the promises of God with the action we are asked to take but must be prepared to take him at his Word believing that all things will work out according to his purposes Heb 11:17-19. Abraham could not share this test with anyone - not Sarah, his servants or his son.

The location of the mountain - Mt Moriah is the area purchased by David to build the Temple 2Sam 24:24,25. Temple Mount (Dome of the Rock) in Jerusalem is of great significance in the present day.

On the third day Abraham and Isaac went on alone - *we will come back to you v5.* Abraham hoped for a change - when you can't see far enough, move ahead and you will see further.

God Himself will provide a lamb for the burnt offering v8. This was a prophetic word by Abraham foretelling the sacrifice of Jesus *the Lamb of God* on the cross on this very location Jn 1:29. At the point of commitment Abraham was stopped. Our responsibility is to obey.

Action by God will always follow when we respond to his request.

Now I know that you fear God – you have not withheld from me your only son v12. It was not that God now knew but that **Abraham now 'knew himself'** – and so must we come to 'know ourselves' - what we are prepared to do for the LORD. His faith had stood the test. Abraham did in effect receive Isaac back from the dead - the son of the promise 17:19; Heb 11:17-19.

The author of Hebrews referred to Isaac as Abraham's one and only son Heb 11:17 – compare this with John 3:16.

22:13-19 On the mountain of the LORD it will be provided - Abraham called the place *YHWH Jireh* Hebrew - the 'LORD will Provide' v14.

Mt Moriah is the location of **Calvary, where God provided His One and Only Son** - the perfect Lamb, sacrificed for the redemption of mankind Rev 5:6-10 - this was a most symbolic event. Abraham was indeed a prophet! 20:7.

In response to Abraham's obedience the blessing was affirmed – the promise of the Savior was for all nations v18.

23:1-20 **Death of Sarah** Sarah was Abraham's partner in the Covenant journey. The local people had great respect for Abraham. He purchased the first plot of land in the Promised Land - the cave of Machpelah.

The Blessing confirmed to Isaac

24:1-67 **Rebecca** The blessing of God applies to all areas of life for those who serve him. Eliezer, chief assistant, was sent back to Abraham's brother, Nahor in northwest Mesopotamia to obtain a wife for Isaac 11:27; 15:2. He was a man of faith – he prayed for success when he reached the location v12. *Before he had finished praying* – God always answers the prayers of those who seek Him v15. Rebecca was granddaughter of Nahor – Eliezer gave thanks to God! v26. Her brother Laban was also a man of belief and accepted the incident as directed by God v50. Isaac was a man of faith – he meditated before the LORD v63. Rebecca became his wife v67.

25:1-18 **Death of Abraham** A brief record is given of the children Keturah bore to Abraham – he lived 175 years. Isaac and Ishmael reunited to bury Abraham with Sarah. Ishmael's record is given before the divine line continued.

Jacob and Esau

25:19-34 Rebecca was barren, then bore twins in response to Isaac's prayer. The LORD gave her a prophetic word – the older will serve the younger v23. Again God's sovereign choice is demonstrated *not by works but by him who calls Rom 9:10-12.* Jacob means 'supplanter' v26.

Birthright was important in the culture of the time. Jacob's request for the birthright showed his knowledge of the prophecy to Rebecca and his determination to obtain the blessing of God v31. Esau showed contempt for the birthright v34. Jacob, as the one who is desperate for the blessing of God contrasts with Esau, the one who settles for the things of this world Mt 5:6.

26:1-35 **Isaac and Abimelech** During famine in Canaan Isaac received instruction not to go to Egypt as Abraham had. The promises made to Abraham were renewed with Isaac v3. Blessing was evident in material things v12-15. Isaac returned to Beersheba where the promises were reaffirmed v24. The local people made an agreement with Isaac. Esau's association with the locals caused grief to his parents v34,35.

The Blessing of Abraham Received by Jacob

27:1-46 As Isaac grew old the time came to pass on the birthright of the family including the Covenant Promises of God. Isaac chose Esau as the firstborn in line for the birthright who was also his favored son. Yet he married foreign women against the wishes of his parents 27:46; 28:8,9. Rebecca had received the prophetic word from the LORD and would have passed it on to Isaac 25:23.

Acting under his natural reasoning, Isaac ignored the prophetic word and did not consult God. Jacob had bargained the right to the birthright because Esau despised it 25:31,34. So Rebecca acted to deceive Isaac and Jacob joined her in the deceit. Isaac was fooled and gave the primary family blessing to Jacob v28,29. When Esau returned Isaac realized that he had been wrong in choosing Esau so he gave him a secondary blessing v39,40. Jacob fled from Esau to Laban the brother of Rebecca in Haran v41-46.

28:1-9 **Isaac's Life of Faith** Isaac is remembered for his acts of faith Heb 11:20. He was prepared to be a sacrifice 22:7,8. He persevered in prayer for a son (over 20 years) 25:21. He continued in his father's beliefs living in tents in a foreign land in order to maintain the family blessing 26:3-6. He finally accepted the blessing of Jacob as the will of God 28:1-4.

The Blessing confirmed to Jacob

28:10-17 Jacob received a dream at Bethel. He saw *a stairway with angels ascending* showing continuous connection between God and the person who seeks him. Despite the obstacles Jacob demonstrated that he valued what God promised – he was desperate for blessing and used every means to be covered by it. We should hunger and thirst for God Mt 5:6. Now God confirmed what Isaac had accepted – the blessing of Abraham would continue through Jacob even to the coming of the Messiah v14. Jacob's response is characteristic of those who seek blessing of God and receive it v17.

28:18-22 Bethel means *'house of God'* – we now have the Holy Spirit with us every moment and may enjoy the LORD's Presence whenever we choose to acknowledge him. We must honor the promises we make. When Jacob had nothing he promised a tenth of everything to the LORD v22.

TWELVE TRIBES OF THE NATION OF ISRAEL

29:1-30 Jacob and Laban Jacob stayed with Laban, the brother of Rebecca, in Haran. He sought to marry Rachel the youngest of Laban's daughters and worked for seven years v15-20. He was tricked into marrying Leah the older daughter v23. We can only ponder this custom. He agreed to work a further seven years for the hand of Rachel v28.

29:31 to 30:24 Twelve Sons Rachel, the favored wife was initially barren. Leah bore six sons – Reuben, Simeon, Levi, Judah, Issachar and Zebulin. Rachel's servant Bilhah bore two sons – Dan and Naphtali. Leah's servant Zilpah bore two sons – Gad and Asher. Rachel then bore a son – Joseph who became Jacob's favored son. These sons together with Benjamin (born to Rachel later 35:18) became the forerunners of the nation of Israel.

30:25-43 Prosperity Jacob worked for wages but after the birth of his children he asked Laban for increased prosperity. God blessed Laban in everything that involved Jacob so he came to an agreement for Jacob to prosper from the livestock – this turned out to be very beneficial for Jacob.

31:1-55 Return to Canaan Jacob's prosperity became a threat. The LORD told him to return to Canaan v3. He departed in stealth out of fear of Laban. The developing faith of the Patriarchs is of example for us. **The LORD reminded** Jacob of his vow. God had certainly fulfilled his part of the agreement v13. Laban set out in pursuit but God told him not to harm Jacob who had served for 20 years. They made a covenant of peace v49.

32:1-23 **Preparing to Meet Esau** In great fear of his brother Esau, despite the presence and promise of God Jacob made physical preparations v7.
Encouraged in Prayer He remembered the promises and goodness of God to him in the past and became strengthened v9-12. We can learn from this model for building our own faith and confidence Ps 103:1-5. When we are faced with difficult situations it is good to spend time alone with God – the LORD will meet with us and provide the guidance, wisdom and encouragement we need Is 40:31. The LORD's Presence continued to be with Jacob.

32:24-26 **Wrestling with God** This encounter in the night rose out of his doubts and fears which often accompany our misgivings. He must overcome them by a positive step of faith - *unless you bless me v26*; 12:4; Ex 7:6; Mt 14:28. Anxiety flees in the face of bold faith Mt 6:25,33.

32:26-32 Jacob persevered in prayer until he received the assurance he sought v26. Often we do not achieve the blessing we seek because we are not prepared to wait on the LORD Ps 46:10; Is 40:29-31. We are required to *be still before the LORD and wait patiently for him Ps 37:7.*
The new name Israel meaning 'strives' was given to Jacob – a name that resounds in the world today.
It is on the basis of God's promise to Abraham & confirmed by this new name given to his grandson Jacob that the present nation of Israel lays claim to their homeland 15:18-21; 35:10. This name and nation will continue to play a significant role in world affairs into the end time Ezk 37:25.
The LORD rewards those who strive to seek him, to understand and carry out his purposes in their lives v28; Hos 12:3-6.
Jacob's encounter with God had an impact on him v30. We have this privilege continually – *we who with unveiled faces all reflect the Lord's glory are being changed into his likeness 2Cor 3:18.*
Jacob bore the mark of his fellowship with God in his body v31.
Jacob's Meeting with Esau

33:1-20 The sight of Esau and his 400 men caused Jacob to take precautions – faith always requires that we use our abilities and resources to achieve the best result. He considered his family would not be harmed. He bowed in humility, with a sense of guilt and fear v3. Esau's reaction put to shame Jacob's anxiety. Faith requires that we believe God even in the worst circumstances v4; Mt 6:25.

Blessing had rested on Esau despite his ways. God is faithful to those who put their trust in Him v9. God's blessing was acknowledged by Jacob v11. Esau sought to be united but Jacob was concerned to be forced into following his brother's worldly ways v13. Jacob moved to Shechem and bought land where he pitched his tent and set up an altar v20.

34:1-31 **Conflict with Shechem** Dinah went out - unprotected. We are in the world but not of it and must keep a distance. Shechem's invitation to conform to the world was not part of God's plan for Israel v12. The trait of deception continued in the action by Jacob's sons. Our actions in the world often prevent our witness and alienate us from those Jesus came to save v30.

Jacob Returned to Bethel

35:1-15 **Promise Renewed** Relocation to Bethel was at God's direction. To grow in our relationship with God requires increased commitment including giving up things which may hinder or stand between us and the LORD. With this comes God's protection and renewal of the promises v11.

35:16-29 **Deaths of Rachel, Leah and Isaac** Rachel died giving birth to the twelfth son Benjamin. The twelve sons became heads of the twelve tribes of Israel v23. Jacob finally arrived back in the land of his father Isaac v27.

36:1-43 **Esau's Descendents** The line of Esau is described before continuing with the divine line of Jacob. Esau's descendents would interact with the people of Israel as the nation of Edom.

JOSEPH, HIS DREAMS and TRIALS – a Great Leader

37:1-36 **PERSONAL VISION** Joseph, eleventh son of Jacob showed a better character and was preferred by his father. He had two dreams about leadership – which became the **vision for his personal life** v5.
A vision is vital to success - to see the end from the beginning - what we want to be, where we want to be and when! We need a vision for our personal life and for every worthwhile activity. Vision becomes the focus and a motivating force to drive towards the result Prov 29:18. It was Joseph's vision established in his dreams that carried him through his hardships.
The jealousy of his brothers was due to many factors – character, preference, ambition Act 7:9. Joseph had the task of reporting on his brothers v13. Bitterness brought about evil intent – *don't let the sun go down on your anger Eph 4:26,27.* Joseph was sold to Ishmaelites – relatives through Abraham! How far the separation had gone v28.

The brothers deceit brought their father grief v31-34. Joseph was age seventeen at the time v2.

38:1-30 **Judah and Tamar** The Bible shows the unpleasant side of the lives of the Patriarchs as well as the good. This event is contrasted with the character of Joseph.

Joseph's Great Test.

39:1 **UNDER AUTHORITY** Joseph was sold into the house of Potiphar, captain of Pharaoh's guard. These testing events were preparing Joseph – he learned to come under authority which must be experienced to be exercised. Our circumstances are always part of God's preparation for greatness 50:20.

39:2-6 **DILIGENT** The LORD was with Joseph and he prospered. He learned diligence by being in service. He also learned and mastered Egyptian. We must **always look for opportunity and take it** when it comes. Because of God's blessing on Joseph Potiphar gave him responsibility over all things.

39:7-20 **INTEGRITY BEFORE GOD** The great test for Joseph came when he was tempted by Potiphar's wife**.** Joseph **proved his integrity** by refusing the temptation. It was against God that he saw the sin v9. Joseph was put in the king's prison through no fault of his own v20.

39:21-23 **PERSISTENT** Joseph prospered in the prison because he **was persistent** in all circumstances and continued to be **faithful to God**. **TASK ORIENTED** Whatever skills Joseph may have had or developed in Egypt his primary goal was to please God. Issues took second place. He was task oriented - he focused on the task at hand regardless of the situation. He did not let circumstance or his feelings get in the way of the task. Whatever he did, he worked at it with all his heart, as working for the LORD Col 3:17,23.

40:1-23 **He was put in charge of the prison** Two officials of Pharaoh's court, cupbearer and baker were imprisoned - this was a vital part of Joseph's apprenticeship. They had dreams which Joseph interpreted. He acknowledged God as the source of his abilities v8. Joseph's request to be remembered shows his desire to be released - but the cupbearer forgot v21-23.

Joseph's Promotion

41:1-57 **Pharaoh's Dreams** That two years passed without despair shows Joseph's patient trust in God. At last his faith was rewarded as he was called before Pharaoh v14. Again Joseph acknowledged God as the source of his abilities v16. God had a plan for Joseph but also acted in the interests of Egypt in the approaching famine v25. Joseph was promoted to second in Egypt – from prisoner to Prime Minister - in fulfillment of his vision v40.

How much did Joseph suffer in the 13 years of trial as God prepared him for greatness? He named his firstborn Manasseh – *God made me forget all my troubles*. His second son he named Ephraim – *God made me fruitful in the land of my suffering v51,52;* Acts 7:10.

Joseph was 30 years old when appointed Prime Minister and lived to 110 years. During this period 1670-1590 BC the Hykos Semitic shepherd kings ruled in Egypt 1700-1500 BC.

41:37-57 **PLAN FOR THE FUTURE** God had provided Pharaoh with a plan to address the coming famine but it had to be developed in detail and managed by a capable person v37-40. A plan is essential in all activities. It sets down what we must do and when. It identifies the steps we must take - how things will be done, what we will need, who will do what, how long each step will take and what it will cost. A plan gives the best chance of achieving our object with the least cost and in the shortest time. Prepared at the beginning it provides a means of measuring progress and a tool for change or improvement. It is a means of communicating and obtaining contribution of others Lk 14:28-33. Plan your activity - your day, week and life.

THE PEOPLE OF ISRAEL IN EGYPT

42:1-38 **Servant of His Family** Famine in Canaan became so severe that Jacob sent his ten sons to Egypt to buy grain. When the brothers appeared before him, Joseph remembered his dream – his vision that had sustained him through his time of preparation v8.

Why did Joseph not seek his family before this? Why did he conceal himself from the brothers? We can assume he waited on God's time to assure the unity of the family would be restored.

Joseph retained Simeon and demanded that Benjamin be brought on the next visit. His purpose was to ensure that Jacob would eventually come to Egypt.

43:1 to 44:34 The famine continued as God worked out his plan. Perhaps Joseph's actions regarding the return of the silver on the first visit and the silver cup on the second were to discipline his brothers for the way they treated him. However they were not done with malice 42:24; 43:30.

45:1-28 GOD'S SOVEREIGNTY - in every area of our lives
Joseph's emotion at seeing his brothers overcame him. He showed character by reassuring them. He acknowledged his suffering as part of God's plan for Israel – *God sent me ahead of you to preserve for you a remnant on earth and to save your lives by a great deliverance* – this was a prophetic word about the future bondage and deliverance of Israel as they became a nation under Moses v7. *It was not you who sent me here but God v8.* We must learn to see God's sovereign plan in all circumstances - *we know that in all things God works for the good of those who love him Rom 8:28.* When we are faithful to follow the LORD even unbelievers respond with favor v16,17.

46:1-34 Jacob in Egypt Jacob at age 130 committed his journey into Egypt to the LORD and received confirmation that this was all part of God's plan – the people of Israel would *learn obedience through suffering* in Egypt before returning to the Promised Land v4; Heb 5:8. Jacob's family, the sons of Israel consisted 70 persons (five in Egypt) 46:8.

47:1-12 With the consent of Pharaoh they settled in the land of Goshen, district of Rameses with other shepherds.

47:13-31 FAITHFUL MANAGEMENT of the Famine All land and property came under Pharaoh's control during this time. Joseph had faithfully served Potiphar, Pharaoh, Egypt, his family and his God.

AN EXAMPLE OF A GREAT LEADER
1. A Personal Vision 37:5-7
2. Working under Authority 39:1
3. Diligent in Service 39:5
4. Integrity before God 39:9
5. Persistent in all Circumstances 41:39
6. Recognize the Sovereignty of God in all areas of Life 45:8
7. A Servant Leader at all Times 47:20

We can gain great value by practicing the skills and attitudes of Joseph, in our personal and professional lives as well as in our service for the LORD.

THE SERVANT LEADER MODEL set down by Jesus and demonstrated by Joseph is recognized in the world as Servant Manager Mt 20:25-28; Jn 13:12-17. Jacob arranged to be buried in the land of the promise showing his belief in God's Word 47:29-31.

***48:1-22* The Blessing Passed On** Jacob included Joseph's two sons in the covenant blessing as an act of faith v3-5; Heb 11:21. The younger received the greater blessing – spiritual blessing does not always follow the natural line v14.

49:1-33 Jacob blessed each of his twelve sons from first to last. **Messiah** - Judah, the Lion of Judah, inherited the line of future kings leading to Jesus, the Messiah – *until he comes to whom it belongs and the obedience of the nations is his v10*; Ezk 21:26,27 – *the Lion of Judah, the Root of David has triumphed Rev 5:5.*
Jacob died at 147 years of age 47:28.

***50:1-26* God intended it for good** How did Joseph deal with the disappointments, resentments and frustrations of his ordeal? He held to the word God had given him - despite all the difficulties and changing circumstances of his life he knew that God intended it for good v20. This is the foundation principle for faith and hope and can transform our lives if embraced Rom 15:13.
Jacob's embalmed body was buried in Machpelah with Abraham.

Again Joseph's character was manifested – the brother's fears of payback were not justified - *you intended to harm me but God intended it for good v19.* We believe God has every step of the way in his hand Ps 139:16. It is a great encouragement in the circumstances of life to trust him for the outcome. May we learn to see the purpose behind the things that happen.
Joseph died age 110 years v26. Despite his fame in Egypt he wanted his body returned to the land of promise – an act of faith Heb 11:22.

Conclusion - The Book of Genesis ends with God's people, the children of Israel in Egypt ready to be brought by the mighty hand of God into the Promised Land.

Exodus – 'going out'

Introduction - The Israelites moved to Egypt as free people in the time of famine where Joseph had become Prime Minister about 1670 BC. Over the next 150 years they were enslaved because of the threat to Egypt of their increasing numbers and origin. At the right time God intervened to deliver them with a mighty hand under the leadership of Moses after ten plagues and the crossing of the Red Sea around 1446 BC. As they left Egypt they celebrated the Passover, a foretaste of the coming of Jesus. In six weeks they came south to Mt Sinai where they received the **Ten Commandments and instructions for the Tabernacle – the Tent of Meeting**. They remained there for one year to build the Tabernacle and institute the order of worship and civil life ordained by God.

Author – Moses wrote down all the instructions God gave him on Mt Sinai 24:4. He was skilled in the ways of the Egyptian royal court. His authorship was confirmed by Jesus Mk 7:10; 12:26; Lk 20:37; Jn 5:46,47; 7:19-23.

Period – From the birth of Moses to the dedication of the Tabernacle and establishing the order of worship at Mt Sinai – a period of 81 years. The Exodus took place when Moses was 80 years of age. The journey to Mt Sinai took six weeks. The people camped at the base of Mt Sinai for ten months till the Tabernacle was built and commissioned. They departed from Mt Sinai after a further six weeks – thirteen months after leaving Egypt.

Theme – From bondage to nationhood God promised Abraham that his descendants would become a great nation Gen 12:2. In Exodus we see the supremacy of the LORD God demonstrated by delivering Israel from Egypt and his provision in bringing them to Mt Sinai.

The Covenant for establishing the nation of Israel was instituted in the giving of the Ten Commandments, the civil law and the form of worship. From this we learn much about the nature of God and our approach to him – also that he can be trusted in all circumstance.

Another theme of Exodus is the Plan of Redemption – through the Passover and the crossing of the Red Sea 1Cor 5:7. The purpose of the Tabernacle was to represent the Presence of the LORD always among his people. His plan is to redeem a remnant of mankind for his eternal kingdom -

• **The Passover** signified that the people were being rescued out of slavery (bondage) to belong to God. In the same way we are brought out of bondage to the world and the devil by the sacrifice of Jesus Col 1:13,14

- **The Red Sea Crossing** signified separation from the old way of life. So in Christ our sins are washed away, we die to the old way of life and enter a whole new way - the old has gone, the new has come Col 3;1-4.

Egyptian Secular History – While the names of the Pharaoh's in Genesis and Exodus are not stated it is informative to consider the Egyptian records which are supportive of the situations in the Bible account -

- The Hyksos Semitic kings ruled Egypt from Avaris in the east of the Nile Delta at the time of Joseph and the arrival of Jacob in Egypt around 1700-1500 BC
- They were expelled by Ahmose who ruled the New Kingdom from Thebes in the south 1540-1525 BC – a new king who did not know about Joseph 1:8
- Hatsepsut, daughter of Pharaoh Thutmose II, ruled Egypt around 1504-1482 BC during the early years of Moses
- Akhenaten, Pharaoh from 1352-1336 BC rejected the old (failed) gods of Egypt, became monotheistic, worshiping the sun (Aten) and moved the capital to Armana
- After his death the priests returned to the old gods.

SUMMARY
The People of Israel in Captivity 1:1 to 2:25
The Encounter with YHWH 3:1 to 4:31
Moses Before Pharaoh 5:1 to 11:10
The LORD's Passover 12:1 to 13:22
Departure from Egypt 14:1 to 15:21
Journey from the Red Sea to Mt Sinai 15:22 to 18:27
The Covenant Presented 19:1-25
The Ten Commandments 20:1 to 24:18
The Tabernacle 25:1 to 31:18
Failure to Keep the Covenant 32:1-35
The Presence of the LORD 33:1 to 34:35
The Tabernacle Completed 35:1 to 40:38

THE PEOPLE OF ISRAEL
1:1-6 **The Twelve Tribes of Israel** Jacob's sons became the forefathers of the nation of Israel. They migrated to Egypt in the seven

years of famine – seventy five in all Acts 7:14. They were there four generations from Jacob to Levi, Kohath, Amran and Moses Ex 6:16-20; Gen 15:16.

The period from the promise to Abraham until the giving of the Law on Mt Sinai was 430 years – six generations including Isaac and Jacob. If we consider 25 years for Abraham (from 75 to 100 years old), allow some 65 years for each of 5 generation with 80 years for Moses at the Exodus this becomes 430 years Gal 3:16, 17 (ref p94).

(An alternative understanding is that Israel was in Egypt 430 years Ex 12:40,41 - not 215 years (a difference of 215 years). Paul described the time from the giving of the promise to Abraham until the giving of the Law as 430 years Gal 3:16,17 (ref p94)).

The time in Egypt from the death of Joseph to the Exodus was 144 years. The Temple was begun by Solomon in his fourth year as king 966 BC - 480 years from the time Israel came out of Egypt 1Kin 6:1. The Bible date for the Exodus is 1446 BC. The promise was given to Abraham 1876 BC.

1:7-22 **The people multiplied** under the blessing of God. Pharaoh's name is not mentioned – he was not relevant to the narrative! The 'store cities' may have predated Rameses.

The people were oppressed v11 Why does God allow adversity? Difficulties are required to establish character and leadership ability – *although he was a son he learned obedience from what he suffered – once made perfect Heb 5:8*; 1Pet 1:7. God brings adversity to develop trust and faith. He moulded and shaped the people then as he does with each of us. God would reveal His glory to Israel and Egypt to prepare Israel as a great nation Gen 15:12-21.

There is no limit to the evil in the heart of sinful mankind v22.

God may require great sacrifice but we must be faithful to the one who called us – we cannot see the final outcome Acts 7:60; 8:1.

The Birth and Training of Moses.

2:1-10 **Moses Parents** Amran and Jochebed 6:20 are among the heroes of faith Heb 11:23. They hid Moses for three months because they believed that God intended a future for their son. They were recognized for their faith – believing what God had told them. The presence of the sister showed the expectation of faith v4. God's providence was clear - the training Moses would need to lead Israel could not have been gained as a slave v5. Moses means 'draw out', an Egyptian name v10 (compare with Ra-meses).

***2:11-15* Moses failed plan** *Moses was educated in all the wisdom of the Egyptians and was powerful in speech and action Acts 7:22.* He was most capable to lead the people through the wilderness and also to record and collate the Books of the Law. He showed an affinity with the Israelite people – he would have known of his connection through circumcision. As adopted son of Pharaoh's daughter he was in an ideal position to help them Acts 7:22. But he made decisions based on personal position, ability and emotions. He was impetuous and presumptuous. His plan to intervene was not God's plan – he was only half way through his training. The bitterness of the people as slaves is clear v14.

Did Moses flee out of fear or did he choose to go? Heb 11:24-27. Sometimes our convictions and actions lead us to do things that are not easy. His rash actions had freed him for the next stage of preparation.

***2:16-22* Moses in Midian** They were descendents of Abraham Gen 25:1,2. (Reuel v18 cf. Jethro 3:1). Moses resided with Jethro and married Zipporah. He named his son Gershom 'an alien' – indicating his sense of failure. Disappointment and hardship rightly understood prepare future leaders. The greatness of Moses lay not in his position in Egypt but in his willingness to submit his abilities into the hand of God in answer to his call.

2:23-25 God heard their cry God always hears. Sometimes we feel like God is remote. However we know that He is always with us and working for our best interests Rom 8:28.

God has a plan for each life He places each person in a position for a purpose. We may not understand the detail at the time. He always intervenes in our circumstances at the right time. No matter how difficult the task it will be achieved when we bring our abilities into line with God's will Jos 1:8; Jer 29:11-13.

ENCOUNTER WITH YHWH – Moses at the Burning Bush

3:1-4 The 40 years Moses spent in the desert were a time of great refinement. The LORD appeared in a burning bush. God seeks to get our attention by the circumstances of life.

When the LORD saw that Moses drew aside The LORD had chosen Moses - now Moses must choose God. He speaks when he sees he has our interest v4. We need to respond in little things if we are to be used in great ways.

3:5-11 Do not come any closer The holiness – 'separateness' of God is first revealed in this encounter. We are now called to draw near Heb 10:22!

I am the God of your fathers Abraham, Isaac and Jacob God revealed Himself as the God of the Covenant v6 and of the living Mt 22:32.

I have indeed seen - I have heard them - so I have come down to rescue them v7,8. This is our God who sees all, hears all and who redeems.

The land of promise was described as *flowing with milk and honey.*

Now go, I am sending you God often calls us outside our comfort zone v10.

Who am I? Moses' reluctance reflected his current inadequacy, past failure and fear of Pharaoh v11. He was being called to be a partner with God. Doubt must be removed - faith must be developed before he could be used for the task ahead. Self-sufficiency was gone - inadequacy qualifies for effective service - humility made him ready. Faith is the key to all the treasures of God's promises - mental assent alone will never give them substance in our lives.

We may feel like Moses, inadequate for a task. Never doubt the call of God on your life. Humility is the quality that makes one qualified in the service of the LORD Is 57:15; Mk 9:33-50; Jas 4:6,7.

3:12 I will be with you - (Hebrew *eheyh*) Moses will not go alone - he is an ambassador - the King will go with him 2Cor 5:20. This promise of God's Presence is to all who will respond to Him Mt 28:20. A deeper relationship develops in the midst of commitment.

You will worship Me v12 God's intention is always that we may experience his Presence and give him the worship that is due to him.

3:13 What is your name Moses required further confirmation of God's Person so that the people might believe him.

FURTHER REVELATION OF THE NATURE OF GOD

3:14 I AM WHO I AM - (Hebrew *Ehyeh Asher Ehyeh).* Compare this expression with the name LORD God - (Hebrew *YHWH Elohim*) Gen 2:4-6. The expression 'Ehyeh' sounds like 'YHWH' – a play on words. It gave added meaning to the name YHWH describing the Covenant name of God and his unique relationship with mankind. Together these words mean **'I AM, present - with all that I Am - for you'**.

This was a further step in the self-revelation of God and his nature describing his active Presence to be with and for his people - **I reveal who I am by what I do** 20:2. This means YHWH is not part of the physical universe but independent, unlike the gods of the world. Yet he is not remote from it and is also active in the world for his people.

Revelation of the nature of God At this point we may review the progressive revelation of God as reinforced by subsequent events Gen 14:21-24 (ref p22) –

• **He is self-existent** – He has his being of himself Gen 1:1; Is 40:25,26,28 – the only application of eternal.

• **He is complete, absolute, unlimited** – without beginning or end Ps 90:2 – the only explanation for existence

• **There is no existence beyond or apart from Him** - I AM and there is none else (no god) besides Me 1Sam:2:2; Is:45:5,6

• **He knows all things, sees all things** – He is omniscient Ps 139:1-5; 1Jn 3:20 – knows all things past & future!

• **He is present in all places** – He is omnipresent Ps 139:7-12. Immanent – all pervading, indwelling Jer 23:24. Transcendent – above all and in all Acts 17:28

• **He possesses all power** – He is omnipotent Ps 139:13-18. All power and energy come from him Mt 19:26; Is 45:6-8; Gen 18:14

• **He is the source of all things** - all else have their being from God and are wholly dependent upon him. He created all things and upholds all things by the word of his power Col 1:15-17; Heb 1:1-3

• **He is eternal and unchangeable** Gen 21:33 - always the same, yesterday, to-day and for ever Heb 1:10-12; 13:8; Rev 4:8. He is faithful and true to all his promises, unchangeable in his person, nature and Word Jas 1:17

• **He is incomprehensible** - we cannot by searching find him out – only as He reveals himself Is 55:8,9

• **He is personal** - His Presence is active in a personal way with and for his people. He is actively engaged in every part of his creation and the affairs of mankind - he directs history Gen 2:7; 3:8

• **He is Spirit** – His spiritual invisible nature is more fully revealed by Jesus and the Holy Spirit Gen 1:2; Jn 3:3-8; 4:23,24; 14:15-20

• **His nature and character are moral** – he is holy, goodness, grace, love, mercy, truth, righteousness, justice, compassion. He is the altruistic, self-giving 'agape' love - who gives not because of the object or response but because of the source – *God is love 1Jn 4:8*. This love is fully revealed in the cross of Jesus. Man is made in the 'image of God' having the best traits and qualities as a reflection of the absolute nature and character of God. Evil is a result of mankind's departure from God. As God has given to mankind physical life, so he offers spiritual, eternal 'God-life' through Jesus.

***3:15-22 The LORD (YHWH Elohim) the God of your fathers sent
me - this is my name forever** v15;* Gen 2:4-7. Moses must revive among
the people the faith of their forefathers which was almost lost and then
they might expect the promises made to their forefathers. The LORD
keeps those who serve him always in his Presence v16.
The elders will listen to you God prepared the way for Moses from the
beginning. He knows all things and always acts to achieve his purposes
in the world and in our lives v18-20.

4:1-17 Signs for Moses He was gripped by reasonable doubt. ***What
is in your hand? v2.*** God takes what we have and are willing to offer to
him and will use it for his purposes – even a staff, the symbol of Moses'
skill. God always backs up his requests with the necessary provision - the
staff, then the leprous hand and some water from the Nile v6,9; Phil 4:19.
***I am not eloquent** v10* Moses had to learn that it was not his ability but
what God could do with him – a lesson and encouragement for all who
will serve him. Continued reluctance displeases the LORD – he has
other means at his disposal v14. Moses' staff now became the **'Staff of
God'** his greatest asset! v16,20. God's instructions were clear. Why did
Moses hesitate? When you have concerns move as far as you can - then
you will see further.
The reluctant shepherd was about to become the great leader.

4:18-31 Moses returned to Egypt God was about to demonstrate to
Israel that he has absolute power and they could trust him. He would take
them from slavery to nationhood.
***I will harden the heart of Pharaoh** v21.* It is not natural to think that
Pharaoh should be guilty if God hardened his heart. It is clear that
Pharaoh did not want to release his slaves. However God's sovereign
purposes are above our understanding Is 55:8,9. We can rest in the
assurance that his purposes are right and his grace is complete. *It does
not depend on man's desire or effort but on God's mercy Rom 9:16-
18.* God intervened in the affairs of his people – he prepared Moses,
called him, gave him instructions and power, hardened Pharaoh and
then delivered the people. All of this was God's doing. We learn that the
God we serve is One who intervenes in the lives of his people for good
regardless of the situation.
As God chose Abraham, he also chose the nation of Israel as his firstborn
in status and as forerunner of those to come – who believe in Jesus!

v22; Gal 3:29. An interlude shows the importance of obedience and commitment to the LORD v24.

The people believed that the LORD would deliver them and they worshiped. Helpless slaves were about to become a great nation v31.

Moses before Pharaoh

5:1-23 **The LORD, the God of Israel** – a formal name of God that Pharaoh would understand. Unbelievers will not acknowledge God despite signs and warnings v2.

The vindictiveness of human nature is again clear v6.

Make the work harder v9 This was the first of many tests for Moses. In the face of expected success he met disaster. Egypt is synonymous with the world. We must learn that things do not always go to our plan and that God has a greater purpose. We can look back & see that there was a reason. When no one is there - trust God!

How quickly we turn in the face of adversity. Many times the people grumbled and were ready to give up – if they had they would have missed out on their destiny v21. When we set out to do what God asks do not expect immediate results or that people will applaud you. In fact it is often the opposite. When things do not go well turn to the LORD – he is in control. Bring your doubts, fears, disappointments and uncertainties to him v22; 1Pet 5:7.

God's Promise Renewed

6:1-30 Now you will see Action was proceeding to God's plan - worldly resistance is necessary for God to demonstrate his sovereign power. In the midst of difficulties, frustrations and despair God directs us to his outcome.

I am the LORD - YHWH v2 – the covenant name is compared with the name **God Almighty - *El Shaddai*** revealed to Abraham Gen 17:1. The Covenant with Abraham was being outworked as God prepared to redeem the people to be his own v6,7; 3:7,8.

Moses and Aaron (family of Levi) were now the leading figures v14.

Judgment on Egypt

7:1-7 **Moses returned to Pharaoh** The stubborn hearts of those who will not submit to the existence and mercy of God is seen v3.

I will lay my hand on Egypt v4 The purpose of the plagues was twofold: to demonstrate the supremacy of God to Israel and to bring judgment against the gods of Egypt. Each plague corresponded to one of the many Egyptian idols 12:12.

7:8 to 10:29 **Signs, Plagues, Blows** The duration of the plagues was possibly one year. The plagues show God's sovereignty over man and nature and Pharaoh's unyielding heart v14 as he acts to redeem his people.
Plague 1 – *the waters of the Nile 7:17* sacred to Egypt. After each plague Pharaoh was given opportunity to change his mind v23.
Let my people go so that they may worship me 8:1 – the importance to God of the worship of his people is clear 3:12.
Plague 2 - Frogs 8:2 – the consequence of the contaminated water.
Plague 3 - Gnats 8:16 – the first sign the Egyptians could not reproduce – there is a limit on human ability and on evil.
Plague 4 - Flies 8:21 *I will make a distinction* – God always wants to make His people distinctive from the world v22,23.
Plague 5 - Livestock 9:1 – the livestock of Egypt became diseased and died – a blow against their wellbeing.
Plague 6 - Ash became boils 9:9 The Egyptians were struck with sores – a blow against their comfort.
Plague 7 - Hail - from the sky so severe that all it fell on were killed 9:18 – a blow against their security.
Plague 8 - Locusts - that covered the land and filled the houses 10:4.
Plague 9 - Darkness that could be felt covered Egypt for three days 10:21 – yet the Israelites had light where they lived 10:23 – they were differentiated from the Egyptians to emphasize the blow.
Severity of the plagues We may wonder at the extent of the plagues but there was purpose in everything. *I have raised you up for this very purpose that I might show you My power and that My name might be proclaimed in all the earth 9:16.* In each event there was opportunity for Pharaoh to recognize the will of God but he stubbornly refused. Many people continue to deny the hand of God in their lives to their determent. Pharaoh agreed for the people to go with conditions - we cannot set conditions on our obedience 10:24. It was Pharaoh's decision to pronounce death 10:28.
The Spoiling of Egypt
11:1-10 **Plague 10 – Death of the first-born** The people were told to plunder the Egyptians – the LORD always provides for those who obey him - wages for their time in captivity and provision for the journey v2.

Every firstborn son in Egypt will die v5 Pharaoh enslaved God's people
– now they would be released.

Again the people were spared. They needed to know the LORD acts
differently with His people to those of the world – He expects them to
act differently to the people of the world v7.

THE LORD'S PASSOVER

12:1,2 **A New Beginning** Israel were to become a new nation so this
day marked the first month (Nisan) of the first year of **their new calendar**
– their sacred year. They still retained the previous first month (Tishri)
as the beginning of their civil year (six months later).

12:3-30 **The Passover sacrifice** *Take a lamb* - the lamb was brought
into the house and cared for. It had to be a year old and without blemish
v5. It was sacrificed on the fourteenth day at dusk as a substitute –
foreshadowing things to come v6.

Blood was smeared on the doorframes as a symbol v7.

The same night the meat was roasted and eaten with bread made without
yeast (representing sin) and bitter herbs to signify their suffering in Egypt
and that they would leave Egypt in haste v8-11.

I will bring judgment on all the gods of Egypt v12 Judgment came
on Egypt and Pharaoh, the monuments and self images, gods and sun
worship. Judgment will come on all that stands against God.

I will see the blood and pass over you v13. Emphasis is on the covering
– as atonement for sin.

In future the Passover would be celebrated each year on the 14th day
of Nisan to remind the people of this mighty deliverance. They were to
celebrate, for this was the day the LORD delivered them out of bondage
v17. It would be followed by a time of thanksgiving for seven days as the
Feast of Unleavened Bread v14,15,17.

Significance of the Passover The Passover foresaw the need and means
of atonement for sin by the substitution of a sacrifice for the people 30:10;
Lev 16:1-34.

The Passover was a shadow of the coming of Jesus - *Christ our
Passover lamb has been sacrificed 1Cor 5:7.* We are redeemed *with the
precious blood of Christ, a lamb without blemish or defect 1Pet 1:19.*
Believers are covered by the blood of Jesus shed on the cross and so
pass from death to life through the forgiveness of sins - the blood makes
atonement – removes the offense to God Lev 17:11.

12:31-51 Up! Leave - Go, worship the LORD After ten plagues Pharaoh told Moses to leave with the people v31. This fulfilled the 430 year promise to Abraham Gen 12:1-4; Gal 3;17. They just had to walk out of bondage!

13:1-16 **Consecration of the Firstborn** This reminded the people of the special place they held as the LORD's firstborn among the nations. They were to bring their children up to honor God as their deliverer v14.

13:17-20 There was a shorter route to the land of promise but they were not ready for conflict v17. They were also not prepared as a nation by the time at Mt Sinai. The embalmed body of Joseph was taken back to the Promised Land as requested - an act of faith v19. They left Succoth on the edge of Goshen and moved south to Etham on the northern tip of the Gulf of Suez (ref p91).

13:21,22 **The Presence of God** was represented by a pillar of cloud by day and fire by night. God will lead us in everything we do – the pillar prefigured the coming of the Holy Spirit whose lead we must follow Jn 14:16; Gal 5:25.

DEPARTURE FROM EGYPT

14:1-31 **The Final Victory** There was one more blow to come against Egypt - *I will gain glory for myself v4.*

They were terrified and cried out v10 How quickly the people forgot what God had already done for them. That is why our faith must be tested repeatedly to prove that it is genuine 1Pet 1:7. They were led to the limit of human ability to help them place trust in God's power and provision. *Do not be afraid. Stand firm and you will see the deliverance of the LORD v13.* In every situation we can be confident God will provide as **we stand firm on his Word and promises** – he will fight for us v14. We put our requests to God and move forward in anticipation of the answer v15. Moses had now come to the position of faith and trust v21,22; 3:11.

The people put their trust in the LORD v31 When they saw the great power the LORD displayed. This is the outcome of faith building. They were now free of Egypt. We want to see a miracle to confirm our belief but *we are commended to God by our faith Heb 11:2:* Jn 20:29. Despite this evidence and profession of faith they were soon to become doubters again.

Give Thanks to the LORD – in everything 1 Thes 5:16-19

15:1-21 This song of Moses compares with the oldest recorded Ps 90. Also Ps 105 and 1Chr 16:7-36 give a description of the deliverance. It is only right that we praise God for who he is and always give thanks for his abundant provision to us Phil 4:4-7. This leads to a joyful life Ps 103:1-5. Anthropomorphism - attributing human form to God who is Spirit Gen 3:8.

JOURNEY FROM THE RED SEA TO MT SINAI

15:22-25 The bitter waters While the actual location of Mt Sinai is not sure, a possible route for their journey and likely location is shown in the map and chart (ref p91-93). They headed southeast from Egypt to Marah where they faced another test of their trust in God. They had seen the plagues, the pillars of cloud and fire, crossed the Red Sea and yet they grumbled *v24,27.*

When our faith is tested there is always an answer. We must learn to trust that God will not let us down - *faith is being sure of what we hope for and certain of what we do not see Heb 11:1.*

15:26,27 I am the LORD Who Heals You – (Hebrew *YHWH Rapha*) - this promise applies to all *who listen, do what is right, pay attention and keep His decrees v26*; Pro 3:5-8. Not only does God promise to keep us from sickness – he also provides healing of our wounds Mt 8:16,17.

The Provision of Manna, Quail and Water

16:1-36 They continued south to Elim into the Desert of Sin - again they complained about lack of food. *You have brought us out to starve v3.* Faith is based on who God is and our relationship with Him. *I will test them and see if they will follow my instructions v4* The whole purpose of testing is to see if our faith, trust and obedience are genuine and to cause our faith to develop.

The glory of the LORD appeared v10 Quail came in abundance – the normal response to faith. Manna, a flake, served to remind the people that God always will supply all our needs – sufficient for the day v16; Phil 4:19.

The test was to see if they would follow the most simple request so that they could go on to greater things v27,28. The LORD works with us in a similar way. Simple response leads to greater calling and blessing.

17:1-7 **Water from the Rock** The people complained at Rephidim on the Sinai Peninsula and again God provided for them v6.

Defeat of the Amalekites

17:8-16 **Amalekites** were descendents of Esau - nomadic tribes who inhabited the Negeb desert around Kadesh-barnea from Canaan to Mt Sinai. They attacked Israel and Joshua led the battle v8-10; Gen 36:12. This was their first major conflict.

When Moses' hands grew tired v11 This emphasizes the importance of prevailing prayer in the battles we encounter. Prayer brings the power of God into our lives. Joshua was the means of victory, prayer was the power. It is sobering to realize that Joshua may have failed if it had not been for the prayer when we contemplate our own shortcomings in this area.

Write this on a scroll v14 There is evidence of writing in Sinai before 1400 BC. This is the **first mention of Joshua** – as future leader he needed to remember past successes as the basis for future faith and also to understand the power, the privilege and the importance of prayer.

The LORD is my Banner – Hebrew ***YHWH Nissi v15*** God is our 'cover' but he requires that hands be lifted up. Here is our model - prayer, the Word and faith coupled with our best effort! Always acknowledge God as the source of our victories.

Jethro's Visit to Moses

***18:1-12* The family returns** Jethro brought Zipporah, wife of Moses & his two sons from Midian where they had been in safe keeping during the confrontation with Egypt. A priest and worshiper of God he was delighted to hear of the LORD's deliverance.

***18:13-27* The Jethro Principle** Jethro observed the practice of Moses in ministering to the people & gave good advice.

Delegation is a powerful technique in all human activity. People are empowered to grow and reach their full potential. Leaders are then released to use their skills on major issues and in strategic development. Small groups pool their resources to achieve the optimum result in problem solving and body building. Each member has special skills and gifts and a desire to contribute. The small group leader is developed and extended practically in all areas of people management, ministry and training.

Group members make their most significant contribution in a team and are encouraged to enter leadership.

Autocratic leadership wears out the leader and also wears out the people – discourages and de-motivates them v17,18.

THE COVENANT PRESENTED – Arrival at Mt Sinai

***19:1-3* A Kingdom of Priests** On the way to Mt Sinai (Mt Horeb) further miracles occurred – bitter water was sweetened 15:22; manna and quail supplied 16:4,13; water provided from a rock 17:1; the Amalekites defeated 17:8. These events were intended to encourage faith in God's provision as they came to the mountain to learn their true destiny as God's chosen people. They were delivered from bondage to *come on this mountain to worship God 3:12*. They arrived in the third month (a journey of six weeks).

19:4-6 God presented Israel with a Covenant – an agreement where he showed his sovereignty, set down the conditions for them to follow and then gave them the promise v3,5,6.

The contest with Pharaoh was to demonstrate God's sovereignty v4.

You will be my treasured possession v5 This was God's plan from the beginning through Abraham for a chosen people.

Although the whole earth is mine v5 – God has concern for all nations – they will also be responsible to him.

You will be for me a kingdom of priests and a holy nation v6 This was to be a new appointment for them.

Holy - separate, set aside from the common, consecrated 3:5-45; Lev 11:44. God intends to show his separateness through his people to the world Ezk 36:23; Heb 10:14. People have a reticence towards holiness 20:18,19 – it interferes with their freedom.

19:7-25 The People's Response They accepted the Covenant v8.

However within a month the conditions were broken 32:1.

Commitment to God requires personal devotion, reverence, trust, sanctification, consecration and intimacy v21. The people presented before God. Moses went onto the mountain v24; Deu 9:9.

This same role is now offered to those who receive Jesus as Savior - they become priests to serve God 1 Pet 2:9.

THE TEN COMMANDMENTS – The Covenant Conditions

20:1-17 These ten words of the Law - recorded on two tablets of stone reveal the moral character and attributes of God. Rather than being preventative they define the basic principle conditions for a personal relationship - both with God and with fellow mankind.

Four define our duty to God - six outline our duty to others. They negate the effect of original sin resulting from the Fall in the Garden of Eden. These principles were confirmed by the command of Jesus both in truth and in spirit and permeated his actions and teachings Mt 22:37-40. They are reiterated in Deu 5:1-21. They are the foundation of western society from 3,400 years ago!

20:2 **I am the LORD your God** This prelude declares the compound name of God - *Ehyeh YHWH Elohim* 3:15 and so bears full authority and severity. It confirms that because God has delivered the people they should follow his ways. The commandments are to be embraced not because they are laws but because they represent the very nature of God Deu 6:4-9.

• **You will have no other gods before me**
This is a declaration of association by God and requires that nothing come before him in the heart and life of the believer. It is necessary for the believer to put away anything that detracts from commitment to God. The world seeks a polytheistic culture. People pursue gods that can be used but not obeyed. This was the downfall of the Divided Kingdoms of Judah and Israel. It is also the record of the rise & fall of nations.

• **You will not make an idol or bow down to it** An idol is anything that draws one's focus away from God and his Person. *God is Spirit and his worshipers must worship in spirit and in truth Jn 4:23,24.* God offers a personal relationship in which we may encounter him at any time Heb 10:19. To seek physical objects or activities as a substitute for fellowship, communion and worship is an offence that falls short of the spiritual reality of our encounter. It is this dependence on physical experience that robs us of spiritual life and power.

• **You will not misuse the name of the LORD** Respect for an individual and their name is a basic right of common decency expected by everyone. Yet it is common to use the name of God and the Lord Jesus as a swear word, a profane expression. This is associated with the misuse of gender terms and the words holy and blood. **They will not be held guiltless** v7. This profanity shows the individual's inner recognition of God and the rebellion of human nature against him and his nature.

• **Remember the Sabbath day by keeping it holy** One day in seven is set aside to 'remember' the Creator, the reason for which we were created. Man is essentially a spiritual being and needs to refocusing on God Lev 23:1-3. There is also need for physical and mental recreation essential for wellbeing - without it leads to stress, anxiety and depression – common conditions in this day.

• **Honor your father and mother** Respect for the sanctity of family as the basic structure of society is fundamental with the acknowledgement of the unique God-given relationship between father, mother & child. The dignity, sacrifice and knowledge of the older generation is to be valued and maintained Lk 2:51,52.

- **You will not murder** Human life is sanctified, precious to God and so must be to his creatures. The value of human life is central to all civilized societies. We have no power over life to create it or extent it – it is the gift of God. Even to pass judgment on another is discouraged Mt 5:21-26, 38-48.
- **You will not commit adultery** The sanctity of the family unit is to be upheld and protected. Divorce represents the breaking of an agreement with God. Divorce leads to heartbreak & suffering for all involved. Lust leads to degeneration and shame. Mt 5:27-32.
- **You will not steal** Personal property is to be respected - a living is to be earned by honest labor Lk 18:20.
- **You will not give false witness** Honesty, truth and justice are to direct one's conduct - regard others as you do oneself Mt 5:33-37.
- **You will not covet** To desire what is not achievable by honest means breeds bitterness, resentment and leads to evil action - it also shows an ungrateful attitude to God Mk 10:17-23.

Eternal Truths There are a number of Law Codes from early societies dating before Hammurabi, king of Babylon 1700 BC. The Ten Commandments have proven their superiority by the depth & simplicity, the all embracing nature and the longevity of application.

These eternal principles of relationship between God and one's fellow man have not diminished with time - they were reinforced by Jesus Mt 5:17-20. Although they have been the mainstay of societies they have been under attack in all generations, none more so than our own. Human nature always seeks to cast off constraint Ps 2:1-3.

A New Commandment At the Garden of Eden there was only one command Gen 2:16,17. At Sinai there were ten Ex 20:1-17. In Deuteronomy there are 614! The Pharisee's made many more.

Now there is only one again - to love God and others, as Jesus has love us! Jn 15:12.

20:18-21 **Fear of God** is rooted in resistance - reverence produces obedience. The Presence was too awesome, too glorious v18,19. God tests these things v20. The people chose to stay at a distance. They withdrew from their calling to the priesthood and the blessing v21; Deu 5:5; 18:15-19 – to exclude the spiritual is to lose value.

Do not have God speak to us v19 It is possible that the multitude of laws that followed were required because the people refused to respond to the basic requirements of God – love foregoes law.

20:22-26 Requirements for building an altar for worship.

Worship, Social Responsibility and Justice

21:1 to 23:9 **Detailed Rules** explained the Covenant Conditions - required because Moses and Aaron were to speak for the people.

Sabbath and Annual Feasts Lev 23:1; Num 28:1; (ref p69)

23:10-13 **Sabbath Rests** A Sabbath rest is to be held each seventh day, month, year and every seventh year. The fiftieth year is also a Sabbath – a time of personal restoration.

23:14-19 **Annual Feasts** There are three annual Feasts -
• Passover and Unleavened Bread, incorporating Firstfruits, combined and held over eight days Lev 23:4-14
• Harvest - Pentecost (Weeks) Lev 23:15-22
• Tabernacles (Ingathering) Lev 23:33-44.
The Festivals of Trumpets and Atonement were not Feasts.

23:20-33 **The Promise of God's Blessing** included food, health, childbirth and full life. These promises apply today and come in response to our worship of God (the angel is surpassed by the indwelling presence of the Holy Spirit in the life of the believer v20). God promises to go before us in the face of opposition v27. Sometimes growth and progress seem slow *little by little* but the result is assured v30.

Their borders would extend from the Red Sea to the Euphrates v31. This occurred under Solomon some 475 years later 2Chr 9:26.

Compromise with the world is a snare to our faith v32,33.

The Covenant Confirmed

24:1-8 The seventy leaders accompanied Moses but only so far. The Presence of the LORD is restricted to those *who seek Him with their whole hearts Jer 29:13.*

Moses wrote down everything v4 - he had the skills of a prince.

The Book of the Covenant confirmed the promises made by God and the conditions required of the people. It had to be ratified by both parties and sealed with blood to emphasize the importance of the agreement v7. The New Covenant was sealed with the blood of Jesus Christ v8; Mt 26:26-28.

24:9-18 **The Glory of the LORD** The leaders had a special glimpse of God to confirm the Covenant. The full revelation was not possible due to the holiness of God Ex 33:20. Moses and Joshua went into the greater Presence – reserved for those who press in v13; Mt 5:8. The doubting people remained in fear at the foot of the mountain v17.

THE TABERNACLE – What was its meaning?

25:1 to 27:21 The LORD instructed Moses to build a tent to represent His Presence among the people. It was also called the **'Tent of Meeting'** 33:7; 40:1-5, 34, 35. *Have them make a sanctuary for me, and I will dwell among them 25:8,9.* It has always been God's purpose to dwell with the people of his choice - first with Adam and then with each of the patriarchs. Now with the descendents of Abraham who were to become the nation of Israel.

The Tabernacle and Courtyard were to be portable to be always with the people during their travels.

How did it work? There were eight stages of approach - corresponding to stages in spiritual growth Heb 9:1-12 -

1. The COURTYARD 27:9-19 - an enclosed quadrangle - 45 x 23 x 2 metres, surrounded by a linen wall with only one doorway entrance.

> † **The Courtyard symbolized that there is only one approach to God** – Jesus said *I am the Door Jn 10:7*

2. The ALTAR 27:1-8 - to make atonement 30:10; Lev 17:11

On entering the outer court the next step was to approach the altar. We must come to God acknowledging his holiness and the offense of our sin to God – seeing it from his side. We repent and seek forgiveness with sincere heart.

> † **The Altar and Sacrifice symbolized salvation through forgiveness** - Jesus said *I am the Good Shepherd, I lay down my life Jn 10:11*

An animal without blemish was sacrificed as a substitute for the atonement of the sin of the individual - *he is to lay his hand on the head of the burnt offering and it will be accepted on his behalf to make atonement for him Lev 1:4.* The sin was figuratively transferred to the sacrifice which was killed – *without shedding of blood there is no forgiveness of sin Heb 9:22.* The sacrifice was offered to God by agreement to remove the offence of sin. The one who offered the animal was forgiven – made right before God. The sacrifice was offered many times including every day, at morning and evening.

Jesus is our sacrifice - once offered, full, perfect, sufficient sacrifice for the remission of sin. When we accept him we are born again by the Holy Spirit. God *rescued us from the dominion of darkness and brought us into the kingdom of the Son He loves, in whom we have redemption, the forgiveness of sins Col 1:13,14.* We know the joy and celebration of sins forgiven and the new birth which could not be obtained by the continual sacrifices Jn 1:12.

But - we must not stay at the altar – we must move on.

3. The LAVER 30:17-21 – water for cleansing, washing every day before approaching the Tabernacle.

How are we cleansed? Daily as we are exposed to the **Word of God** – the scalpel God uses to mould and direct our lives Heb 4:11-13. Progressively *we are transformed by the renewing of our minds Rom 12:2 – being changed into the same image, by the Spirit of God 2Cor 3:16-18.* We are sanctified daily as we come under the influence of the Holy Spirit through God's Word – *be holy because I am holy 1Pet 1:16.*

† **The Laver symbolized sanctification** *I am the true Vine, you are the branches Jn 15:1-3*

4. The TABERNACLE 26:1-37 – the Holy Place - a tent 14 x 4.5 x 5 metres, enclosed with animal-skin and lined with linen – the inner court, sealed from external light. Only priests could enter, consecrated ones given to the duty of the Tabernacle Heb 9:1-7.

Many come to God for the blessing. They camp before the Laver – still in the outer court. They want physical blessing but not the moral cleansing. They are not willing to go on in to His Presence. We must first seek God for who He is and who he wants us to be! Mt 6:33; Heb 5:11-14; 11:6.

† **The Tabernacle symbolized a life devoted to relationship with God** Jesus said - *I and the Father are one Jn 10:30*

5. The LAMPSTAND 25:31-40 – seven candle branches providing continuous light. Outside was natural light. On entering the Tabernacle there was no natural light, only the light of the Spirit.

† **The Lampstand in the Tabernacle symbolized the initial and ongoing filling of the Holy Spirit** Jesus said - *I am the light Jn 8:12*

The Holy Spirit came to walk with us in the same way Jesus walked with his disciples – *to be with us always, to teach, remind, convict and to testify about Jesus Jn 15:26; 16:7-14.* The Holy Spirit came to convict at repentance, to change at conversion and to produce sanctification. But he also wants to fill us. We must acknowledge **his Presence.** A time comes when we must yield our lives to him & learn to walk with him in daily communion – *the grace of the Lord Jesus Christ, the love of God and the fellowship of the Holy Spirit 2Cor 13:14* – then the guidance, direction & power will flow.

Tabernacle Layout & Symbolic Meaning

Courtyard

1. Only one entry
2. Salvation
3. Santification
4. Holy Place
5. Holy Spirit
6. Provision
7. Prayer
8. Presence of God

Holiness

Altar

Bronze Laver

Bread of Presence

Lampstand

Incense

Curtain

Most Holy Place

Ark

45 m

14 m x 5 m

4.5 m

4.5 m

23 m

The Holy Spirit is the **Lord of the Harvest** who directs the work we do Mt 9:38; Acts 13:2. He illuminates the darkness and reveals what is not known. **He is our light, revelation and power** – *since we live by the Spirit let us keep in step with the Spirit Gal 5:25.*

6. The BREAD of the PRESENCE 25:23-30 – 'showbread' - 12 loaves, one for each tribe, replaced every Sabbath. A reminder that **God is the Provider** - present with them to guide, instruct and feed.

† **The Bread of the Presence symbolized that God is our provider in all areas of our life** Jesus said - *I am the Bread of life Jn 6:35* God's Word is our sustenance – *man will not live by bread alone but by every word that proceeds from the mouth of God Mt 4:1-11.* He provides our daily bread – as he provided manna in the wilderness. He is the God of provision and blessing supplying all we need to live for Him and serve Him Phil 4:19. Job treasured God's Word more than his daily bread Job 23:12. David would not neglect God's Word Ps 119:16. This must be our attitude.

7. The ALTAR of INCENSE 30:1-10 – sweet spices offered morning and night

† **The Altar of Incense symbolized our privilege, responsibility and duty to pray** Jesus said *I am the way, the truth and the life Jn 14:6* Daily we offer a sacrifice of praise and thanksgiving to God. We worship, adore and commune with him. We seek guidance and petition him on behalf of others – family, church, community, leaders and nations.

8. The MOST HOLY PLACE 26:31-34 – behind the curtain – 4.5 x 4.5 x 5 metres – shielded from the Holy Place - representing God's Presence where he chose to meet with the people Heb 9:2-5.

† **The Holy of Holies symbolized our fellowship with God – now made available through Christ** *I am the resurrection and the life Jn 11:25*

• **The Curtain** 26:33 shielded God's holiness - the separation of man from God - it was removed by Christ Mt 27:51; 2Cor 3:15,16

• **The ARK of the COVENANT** 25:10-22 - a box of wood overlaid with gold, 1.15 m x 700 x 700 mm containing the conditions of the Covenant – the tablets of the Law.

• **The ATONEMENT COVER** 25:17-22; 30:11; Lev 17:11 – **'mercy seat'** of pure gold, two cherubim, wings touching - a reminder of God's mercy in atoning for sin. It was a cover, not of the Ark, but of the offence of sin Ps 32:1. The propitiation (appeasement), God is appeased by the vindication of his holy and righteous character through the provision he has made in the vicarious (taking the place of) and expiatory (to suffer for) sacrifice of Christ - he has so dealt with sin that he can show mercy to the believing sinner by the removal of guilt and the remission of sins.

† *Christ is our Mercy Seat* Rom 3:25,26

• **The TEN COMMANDMENTS** 40:20,21 – the Ark contained and carried the two tablets of stone – the Covenant conditions - the Testimony of God's agreement with the people -

• the Arc behind the veil **represented God's holiness** -

• the Ten Commandments within **represented the character of God and his requirement for the people** –

• the Atonement Cover above **represented his mercy and forgiveness of sin**

• *There above the cover between the two cherubim that are over the ark of the Testimony – I will meet with you 25:22.*

• **Only the high priest could enter the Most Holy Place - the 'Holy of Holies' - on the 'Day of Atonement'** - to make atonement for the sins of the people, to worship, petition, hear and inquire on behalf of the people - *there I will give you all my commands 25:22.* The high priest was washed, dressed, sprinkled with blood and accompanied by incense – to shield the Presence.

• Atonement was made only once a year for the nation and had to be repeated every year.

† **Jesus ever lives to make intercession for us** Heb 7:25

28:1-43 **Clothes of the Priests** Moses' brother and his descendents were appointed priests to serve before God – responsible for teaching the Law and for decision-making. They wore an ephod (waistcoat), breastplate, robe, tunic, turban and sash. The breastplate contained two stones called 'illumination and truth' or 'decision and judgment' used before God for making decisions and to decide courses of action v30. *Holy to the LORD v36* – everything about the Tabernacle emphasized that God is holy.

29:1-46 **Consecration of the Priests** Bring them to the entrance of the Tent - wash them, dress them with the priestly clothes, sacrifice a bull and two rams - put blood on the right ear, thumb and big toe - sprinkle them and their clothes with blood and anointing oil.

† **This was all symbolic of the present time** Heb 9:8-10

Application of the Tabernacle to the New Covenant -
When Christ came as a high priest of the good things that *are already here – he entered the Most Holy Place once* for all by his own blood, having obtained eternal redemption Heb 9:11,12. His blood was shed, he died in our place - *by one sacrifice he has made perfect forever those who are being made holy Heb10:14.* When he died the curtain was torn from top to bottom Mt 27:51. **The way is open for us to enter the Most Holy Place -** we have confidence to enter - we have a great priest over the house of God - **let us draw near!** Heb 10:19-22. Moses could not draw near! Ex 3:5.

We are a Royal Priesthood This then is the application of the Tabernacle today. We are clothed with the righteousness of Jesus and consecrated through his shed blood - *you are a chosen people, a royal priesthood, a people belonging to God, that you may declare the praises of Him who called you out of darkness into His wonderful light 1Pet 2:9.*

I will dwell among them God's intention is to be with his people 29:45.

    † **Your body is a temple of the Holy Spirit** 1Cor 6:19,20 - we must appropriate the special privilege we have as God's chosen people by our relationship with Jesus and our commitment to serve him

Special Materials and Skilled Craftsmen

30:1-10 **The Altar of Incense** was located in the Tabernacle Holy Place 26:1. Incense was burned each morning and evening as a symbol of prayer. It was also required on the Day of Atonement to shield the Presence v10.

30:1-21 Requirements for atonement money and cleansing of the priests were given.

30:22-38 Requirements for the sacred anointing oil and incense.

31:1-11 Skill, ability and knowledge in crafts were provided by the filling of the Holy Spirit dwelling in the lives of individuals.

31:12-17 Sabbath Day reminded the people of God's provision - time in the Presence produces holiness v13.

31:18 The two tablets of the Testimony inscribed by the finger of God - represented the character of God and his requirement for his people.

FAILURE TO KEEP THE COVENANT - Rebellion

32:1-35 *Come, make us gods v1* While Moses was on the mountain receiving the commandments from God the people who had stood in fear before the mountain forty days earlier were now after the things of the world. To encounter a personal walk with the Almighty requires a persistent commitment to His Presence – who He is and what He requires - in all circumstances.

The choice of a golden calf (or bull) showed the power of past beliefs v5; Jos 24:2. The request of the people for an object to worship in the absence of Moses reveals the shallow nature of the individual's personal relationship with God who is Spirit 20:4.

Afterward they sat down to eat and drink and got up to indulge in revelry v6 The desire to be independent from God is driven by the requirement to cast off constraint Ps 2:1-3. The problem is not one of unbelief but of rebellion.

The weakness of Aaron in the absence of Moses shows the importance of strong leadership.

Judgment came swiftly – it is important to separate from the ways of the world to continue in the blessing of the LORD v27.

Moses returned to the mountain to petition the LORD for a further forty days to seek atonement for the disobedience of the people v31; Deu 9:9,18,25. The consequence of sin is great v35.

33:1-6 Leave this place Moses was told to leave Sinai and go to the Promised Land without the direct Presence of the LORD - an angel would lead them. This was a consequence of the rebellion and to make the people realize the cost of unfaithfulness. Many live their lives without knowing this direct Presence.

THE PRESENCE OF THE LORD

33:7-10 Tent of Meeting Moses had already set a place representing the Presence of God amongst the people as they travelled from Egypt to Sinai.

33:11 The LORD spoke to Moses face to face as with his friend. This is the intimacy that God provides for those who commit to him (the phrase 'face to face' describes intimacy, not physical vision 33:20). As we grow in our relationship with God his Presence becomes more precious. At times he reveals himself more fully as we seek him 1Kin 8:10,11; Is 6:1-9.

The devotion of Joshua for the LORD is also shown v11.

33:12-17 **Moses Met with God** Following the time of intercession and repentance the LORD confirmed that His Presence would go with the people v14. Moses would prefer to stay in the desert where he knew the Presence than to go up to the Promised Land without the Presence v15. *What else will distinguish me* v16 We stand out from the world by our personal relationship with God. Without it we are like all other people. God wants to *show Himself holy through us to the world Ezk 36:23; 37:28.*

33:18-23 A Closer Walk With God After the experience of the burning bush, miracles and plagues, deliverance and parting of the Red Sea, the pillars of cloud and fire to guide, provision of water, quails and manna and the forty day periods on the mountain Moses still wanted to see more of God's glory! This should be our heart's cry Ps 63:1-8 - *blessed are those who hunger and thirst for righteousness for they will be filled* Mt 5:6,8.

Now show me your glory v18 Moses anticipated that there was more to be encountered. One might have expected more demonstration of power but as in the case of Elijah God was not in the great and powerful wind, earthquake or fire but in the still small voice 1Kin 19:11-13. The greater **glory of God** was revealed to Moses in further revelation of his nature - *I will have mercy and compassion v19.*

We may approach God knowing his glory is revealed in ***compassion, grace, abounding in love and faithfulness*** *34:6,7* - ever working for our best interests as we seek to know him and live for him.

A Place Near God Moses could not see God directly v20. However God provided *a place near me where you may stand on a rock where my glory passes by v21.*

We also can know this rock on which we may stand secure from the turmoil of life - where intimacy with the LORD is experienced as we learn to walk with Him in daily communion. We must spend time to seek – with all our hearts - ***teach me your ways that I may know you*** *v13*; Ps 89:15-17.

The Covenant Renewed

34:1-35 The LORD said to Moses If the people were to return to the favor of the LORD it would be under the Covenant Conditions of the agreement. Repentance means returning to the way of the LORD. Two new stone tablets were made to replace those broken by Moses 32:19. The revelation of God continued.

The LORD compassionate, gracious, slow to anger, abounding in love and faithfulness, forgiving - whose name is Jealous v6,7,14 God is passionate in regard to his nature and his ways - he wants his people to be like him and the circumstances of life are provided to achieve this. He is also committed to his people and their wellbeing.

The Covenant relationship and blessings involved total commitment.

His face was radiant v28,29 After the renewal of the Covenant when Moses came from the mountain – his countenance had changed as he spent time with the LORD. This is the experience of all who seriously seek him and spend time in his Presence.

He put a veil over his face v33 The purpose of the veil was to shield the reflected glory. The glory of the LORD is overwhelming for those who do not seek him and so they are shielded. The apostle Paul recognized that the sacrifice of Jesus removed the offense of sin and so there is no separation between God and those who truly seek him. *In Christ the veil is taken away – we with unveiled faces reflect the LORD's glory 2Cor 3:13-18.* As we spend time in the Presence of Christ we are in the process of being changed into his likeness, step by step, by the transforming work of the Holy Spirit. We also reflect the glory of Jesus to others by the way we live.

THE TABERNACLE COMPLETED

35:1 to 40:33 The Tabernacle was set up *just as the LORD had commanded 39:43.*

The work was completed after eleven and half months 40:17.

40:34-38 **The Glory of the LORD** The recommitment of the people was honored by the Presence of the LORD coming among them as a cloud - even Moses could not enter the Tabernacle. This *shekinah* (glory) was a special manifestation of his glory demonstrating to the people that God was pleased with their commitment. His Presence would continue to lead them in all their travels as the cloud of the LORD by day and fire in the cloud by night Ex 13:21.

We can know this Presence of the LORD in our daily lives. He reveals himself in various ways as we serve him, worship him and pursue our relationship with him Mt 28:20.

Conclusion - Israel was now established as the people of God with a national code of worship and conduct. The Covenant initiated with Abraham was in place, they had been disciplined for disobedience and they were equipped to set out to fulfil the promise of God to Abraham that his descendents would possess the Promised Land.

Leviticus – The duties of the Levites

Introduction - At the burning bush Moses was told – when you have brought the people out of bondage you will worship God on this mountain Ex 3:12. Having been delivered from slavery in Egypt they came to Mt Sinai to receive guidelines for becoming a holy nation to represent God to the world.

Author – Leviticus was written by Moses Deu 31:9.

Period – The year the people of Israel camped at Mt Sinai Num 33:2.

Theme - The Holy Nature of God is revealed in Leviticus 10:3; 11:44,45; 19:2; 20:7,26. This presents a problem for us without Jesus, as the soul who sins is the one who will die Ezk 18:4; Gen 2:17; Rom 3:23.

Nations of the World Israel was established in a world dominated by worship of man-made gods. Egypt, Babylon, Mesopotamia, Canaan Jos 23:7; 24:14, in fact all cultures have concepts of a god with human characteristics - sacrifice was required to appease an angry deity. These beliefs were used by the powerful to exploit the weak & keep the people in subjection – without changing the behavior of the individual. Many of the characteristics & practices were immoral.

The Holy Nature of God The God of Abraham, Isaac & Jacob called Israel to be a special people to himself – *out of all the nations* Ex 19:3-6. At Sinai he revealed a code of worship & practice to lift the conduct of the people to a higher level -

• worship was intended to enjoy the presence of God

• offerings were to give back a portion of what God gives to the believer – life, provision & all things

• sacrifice was provided to remove the offense of sin – so serious it required a blood sacrifice.

Holy, 'separate' describes the nature & character of God - absolute qualities of good, righteousness, justice, compassion & mercy Ex 34:6,7. Guidelines revealed the lifestyle required to approach the holy God. The rules were to inspire the people to be holy too – ***you are to be holy to me because I, the LORD, am holy & have set you apart from the nations to be my own Lev 20:26.***

While holiness is required, atonement is provided – it must be embraced.

The Law of the Old Covenant set out the pattern of worship and lifestyle for the people of Israel to prepare a group of slaves to become a nation. It included three areas – moral, social and ceremonial. The ceremonial laws were superseded by the coming of Jesus. The moral laws represent the character of God and still apply. The civil, health and hygiene laws are practical and have largely become part of our culture. The Law impacted every aspect of life.

Aaron and his sons, descendents of Levi were appointed as the priests responsible for the service and care of the Tabernacle Num 1:47-53. A significant part of these instructions was the rules for the priests.

Leviticus is the Book of Atonement It outlines the principles of holiness and the means of atonement by sacrifice. The offense of sin can only be removed by the shedding of blood Heb 9:22. God provided a way to overcome this dilemma by the substitutionary sacrifice of an animal.

The Perfect Sacrifice Animal sacrifice could not remove future sins or the power of sin. God sent his Son Jesus to be the perfect sacrifice for our sin Jn 3:16.

By his perfect life he could offer himself once only, a full perfect and sufficient sacrifice for the sins of those who come to God through him.

- *He sacrificed for their sins once for all when He offered himself Heb 7:27*
- *Christ was sacrificed once to take away the sins of many Heb 9:28*
- *By one sacrifice he has made perfect forever those who are being made holy Heb 10:14.*

Jesus also broke the power of sin Rom 6:6. *How much more will the blood of Christ, who through the eternal Spirit offered himself unblemished to God, cleanse our consciences that we may serve the living God Heb 9:14.*

SUMMARY
Offerings 1:1 to 7:38
Appointment of the Priests 8:1 to 15:33
The Day of Atonement 16:1 to 22:33
Sabbaths and Annual Feasts 23:1 to 25:55
Rewards and Punishments 26:1 to 27:34

OFFERINGS
1:1,2 Offerings were a means of demonstrating response to God in giving thanks or seeking forgiveness for wrongdoing. They were an outward expression of an inner commitment.

There were five offerings, both individual and corporate -

1. Burnt Offering 1:3-17 and 6:8-13 The purpose was to make atonement for the sin of the individual v4 - the animal stood in place of the person.

All offerings involving an animal required the one making the offering to lay hand on the animal and to slaughter it v4. The priest sprinkled blood on the altar and burnt the animal.

2. Grain Offering 2:1-16 and 6:14-23 The purpose was to give a gift of thanksgiving (for the crop) & consecration to the LORD. A portion was burnt to God & a portion retained for the priest.

3. Fellowship Offering 3:1-17 and 7:11-21 The purpose was to fellowship with thanksgiving before the LORD. The fat was burnt & the remainder shared by the priest & person.

4. Sin (burnt) Offering 4:1 to 5:13 and 6:24-30 The purpose was to make atonement for the sin of the priest, person or nation - the fat was burnt & the remainder was for the priest. This sacrifice was also made once each year for the nation at the Day of Atonement.

5. Guilt Offering 5:14 to 6:7 and 7:1-10 The purpose was to make restitution for wrongdoing - the fat was burnt & the remainder was for the priest.

A Shadow of things to come Heb 10:1 These offerings were an example foreshadowing the coming of Jesus - he made a complete offering of himself - without blemish - a substitution for the sinner - to remove the guilt & offense of sin - to restore fellowship between God & man - a cause for thanksgiving Heb 7:26,27; 9:7-15,22,28.

7:22-27 Eating of fat and blood was forbidden.

7:28-38 **The Priest's share** The priest could retain and eat certain portions of the offerings 6:16; 6:26; 7:6; 7:14; Num 18:1-32.

Appointment and Anointing of the Priests

8:1-36 The people met before the Tent of Meeting. Aaron and his sons were washed and clothed with the priestly uniform. They and the Tabernacle were anointed with oil to consecrate them. A bull and two rams were sacrificed. Blood was put on the right ear lobe, thumb and big toe of the priest and sprinkled on the altar Nu 3:1-13.

The Priests began their duty in the Tabernacle

9:1-22 The priests then made atonement for themselves and the people as well as offering the daily services of worship to God.

9:23-24 **Presence of the LORD** On completing the daily sacrifice the LORD appeared in glory confirming acceptance of the service.

10:1-7 **The Holy God** Two sons of Aaron were irreverent and disobedient in service and were consumed by fire v1. *Among those who approach me I will show myself holy – I will be honored v3.*

One cannot presume on the mercy of God.

10:8-20 You must distinguish between the holy and the common
v10. We must show reverence and awe before God and be obedient to his commands. This requires that we separate from the ways of the world in our conduct, thoughts and speech – *be perfect as your Heavenly Father is perfect Mt 5:48.*

***11:1 to 15:33* Food, Health and Hygiene Rules** Many of the Levitical laws were for health and have become part of our culture.
I am the LORD your God, consecrate yourselves and be holy, because I am holy 11:44,45 The nature of God has not changed and we must pursue his holiness in our lives Heb 10:14; 1Pet 1:16.

THE DAY OF ATONEMENT Ex 30:10

***16:1-10* The Presence of the LORD** was represented by the space above the Atonement Cover of the Ark of the Testament between the two cherubim within the Most Holy Place in the Tabernacle. To come into fellowship with the holy God it was necessary for the offence of sins to be removed by shedding of blood. Once each year, on the Day of Atonement, Aaron, as high priest was required to enter the Most Holy Place to make atonement for the sins of the Nation. A bull, two rams and two goats were sacrificed.

16:11-19 He must bathe and clothe, take a censer of incense behind the curtain to conceal the Atonement Cover (so he would not die from the radiant glory) then sprinkle blood on the altar.

***16:20-28* The Scapegoat** One goat was kept alive as a 'scapegoat' v10 – Aaron laid hands on it, confessed the sins of Israel then released the goat in the wilderness – the sins of the people were 'put on' the scapegoat who carried them away v21,22. Jesus became both our sacrifice and our scapegoat – he bore our sins outside the city on Calvary and carried them away.

16:29-34 Then the people would be cleansed of their sins. Atonement was to be made only once a year for all the sins of Israel.

17:1-16 Eating of blood was again forbidden – *for the life of a creature is in the blood and I have given it to you to make atonement for yourselves on the altar, it is the blood that makes atonement for one's life v11,12.*

***18:1-30* The Moral Laws of the Covenant** are fundamental and became the foundation of the western legal system today. We must not conform to the ways of the world but obey the LORD and follow his ways.

***19:1-37* Various Laws** *Be holy because I, the LORD your God, am holy* This is the instruction of Jesus Mt 5:48. Involvement with the spirit world in any form is forbidden v31.

20:1-27 Punishments for sin were prescribed.

21:1 to 22:33 **Rules for priests** emphasized the holiness of God.

SABBATHS, ANNUAL FEASTS Ex 23:10-19; Num 28:1 to 29:40

23:1-3 **The Sabbath Day** The seventh day of the week is a festival to honor God. It is to remind the people they are holy to God. It is also important to have physical and spiritual recreation both of which are essential to the wellbeing of mankind Gen 2:3; Ex 20:8-11.

23:4 **The Feasts and Festivals** (appointed times) to remember God.

There were three annual Feasts Ex 23:14-16; Deu 16:16 -

• **Passover** - incorporating Unleavened Bread and Firstfruits v5-14
• **Harvest** - Pentecost or Weeks v15-22
• **Tabernacles** - or Ingathering v33-44.

There were seven annual Festivals -

1. **Feast of Passover** v5 Instituted at the departure from Egypt Ex 12:1-28 and held annually by a sacrifice on the fourteenth day of the first month of the year, the Day of Preparation reminded the people that God had redeemed them from bondage. The meal was celebrated at twilight, after 6pm. Jesus is our Passover lamb.

2. **Feast of Unleavened Bread** v 6-8 Began on the fifteenth day of the first month with the Passover meal and continued for seven days when bread was eaten without yeast to remind them that they had left Egypt in haste and that they were to be separate from the people of the world.

3. **Firstfruits** v9-14 A sheaf of the first grain harvest was offered in thankfulness to the LORD on the sixteenth day of Nissan - Sunday in Passover week. Jesus rose from the dead on the third day and is the 'firstfruit' of those who will rise again 1Cor15:20-23.

4. **Feast of Pentecost or Feast of Weeks** v15-22 Seven weeks (49 days) after the Firstfruits (Pentecost means fifty) an offering of the new grain was made at the end of the Harvest – associated with Harvest Festival. The Holy Spirit came in fullness at Pentecost.

5. **Blowing of Trumpets** v23-25 On the first day of the seventh month a special celebration was made to remember God's provision.

6. **Day of Atonement** v26-32 On the tenth day of the seventh month atonement was made for national sin with confession and repentance 16:1-34. Jesus provided atonement for our sins at Calvary.

7. **Feast of Tabernacles** v33-44 On the fifteenth day of the seventh month after all the crops of the land were gathered the men lived in tents

for seven days celebrating God's provision on the journey out of Egypt when they had to live in tents in the harsh conditions of the wilderness. Also known as the 'Ingathering' it looked forward as a call to repentance in preparation for the final ingathering at the millennium reign of the LORD Zech 14:1-16.

Relevance - The appointed times looked forward to the Messiah. Jesus died on Passover (14th Nissan) and rose again (16th Nissan) as our 'firstfruit' 1Cor 15:20-23. The Holy Spirit came at Pentecost to empower the Church. We look forward to the return of Jesus.

24:1-4 **The Lampstands** in the Tabernacle required a special formula of sacred oil to keep burning continually Ex 25:31-40.

24:5-9 **The Bread of the Presence** (showbread) one loaf for each of the twelve tribe, was replaced every Sabbath v5; Ex 25:30.

24:10-23 **Blasphemy** The sin of speaking against God, especially against the Holy Spirit was condemned. Human life is to be protected v17.

Further Sabbath Festivals

25:1-55 Each seventh year was a **Sabbath Year** so the land was rested. The **Year of Jubilee** was held on the year after seven Sabbath Years (the fiftieth year) v8. Liberty was proclaimed to all inhabitants – each returned to his own family property and ate only what grew of itself. Purchased land was returned to the inherited owner, slaves and servants were released.

The purpose of the Jubilee Year was to remind the people that the land belonged to the LORD – he had given them each an inheritance and they were his servants; consequently they must be fair and kind in dealing with others.

26:1-13 **Reward for Obedience - Obedience brings blessing** – rain in season, plenty, peace, protection, prosperity, fruitfulness.
This is an encouragement & warning for the world today.

26:14-39 **Disobedience will bring punishment** – rejection of God will result in loss of his favor.

26:40-46 **Repentance brings return of favor** – God's character is to show mercy, forgiveness and blessing to those who repent.

27:1-34 **The importance of commitments** A person's word is to be honored - vows and promises kept.

A tithe of everything from the land belongs to the LORD v30

The Feast of the LORD

Festival	month	day	duration	reference	Ex 23:14-16; Lev 23:1-44; Num 28:1 to 29:40
1 Passover	Nisan	14th day	1 day	Ex 12:2-14	Deliverance from bondage in Egypt
	1st month	Friday		Lev 23:5	Start of the year
	Mar / Ap			Nu 28:16-25	*Christ our Passsover 1Cor 5:7,8*
2 Unleavened	Nisan	15th day	7 days	Ex 12:15-20	Bread with no yeast (no sin)
Bread	1st month	to		Ex 23:15	Remembering they left Egyt in haste
	Mar / Ap	22nd day		Ex 34:18	Jesus died to take away our sins
				Lev 23:6-8	*Live the Festival without yeast 1Cor 5:7,8*
3 Firstfruits	Nisan	16 th day	1 day	Ex 23:16,19	Beginning of harvest
	1st month	Sunday		Lev 23:9-14	First sheaf of barley grain
	Mar / Ap			Deu 26:1-11	Second day of the Passover Festival
					Christ the firstfruit of us 1Cor 15:20-23
4 Pentecost	Sivan	7 weeks	7 days	Ex 23:16	Harvest Festival - thanksgiving for provision
Weeks	3rd month	50 days		Ex 34:22	End of wheat grain harvest
	May / June	after		Lev 23:15-22	Giving of the Law at Mt Sinai
		Passover		Nu 28:26-31	*Coming of the Holy Spirit Acts 2:1-4*
5 Trumpets	Tishri	1st day	10 days	Lev 23:23-25	Blowing of trumpets - year end Harvest
	7th month	to		Nu 29:1-6	Call to reflection & repentance
	Sep / Oct	10th day			Call to the people & nations for end times
6 Atonement	Tishri	10th day	1 day	Ex 30:10	High Priest makes atonement for the nation
	7th month			Lev 23:26-32	Enters the Most Holy Place Rom 3:25
	Sep / Oct			Nu 29:7-11	Scapegoat sent to the desert
					Day of fasting, confession, repentence
7 Tabernacles	Tishri	15th day	7 days	Ex 23:16	Men lived in Booths, Shelters - a reminder of
Ingathering	7th month	to		Lev 23:33-43	God's provision in 40 years of wandering
	Sep / Oct	22nd day		Nu 29:12-39	End of year Harvest - Fruits, olive, grape.
				Deu 16:16	Looked to the coming of Messiah Zec 14:1-16

Numbers – 'numbering of the people'

Introduction - The first nine chapters review the year Israel camped at Mt Sinai in preparation to enter the Promised Land. Chapters ten to fourteen record their refusal to go in to Canaan due to fear of the inhabitants. The remainder of the Book describes their subsequent years of wandering in the wilderness until the whole disobedient generation had died before coming to the east side of the Jordan River ready to enter once more. A possible path of their wandering is shown in the map and chart (ref p91-93).

Author – Numbers was written by Moses 33:2; Deu 31:9.

Period – The journey of the people of Israel from Mt Sinai to the border of the Promised Land for the second time – a duration of 39 years.

Theme – Great Expectations After all the preparation at Mt Sinai the people set out as a nation with pride & anticipation of greatness.

Wandering in the Wilderness In eleven days they arrived at the border of Canaan. They had the opportunity to trust God to lead them into the Promised Land as he had promised but they refused because they were overcome by the magnitude of their circumstances and their own inadequacies. This failure resulted in a 39 year delay in the fulfillment of God's promises and in the death of all those unbelieving adults. Unbelief brings discipline – lack of faith hinders blessing.

Message for today The believer has been brought out of the bondage of sin and the world by the death of Jesus. We too have the opportunity to enter the rest of God Heb 4:1-3,6. We also may embrace all the promises of God and faithfully achieve all that God has prepared for us Eph 3:20. However many miss a calling or opportunity because of failure to take God at his Word. Our desire for security, comfort and the pleasures of the world can prevent us from reaching our potential.

A Second Chance to Enter A census to number the people was taken twice – one before they left Sinai and a second as they came to the end of their wandering and were finally to enter the land of promise 1:2; 26:2.

The love, faithfulness and patience of God are demonstrated as he works out his eternal plan for mankind to prepare a people for himself – a people redeemed and sanctified to spend eternity in his Presence.

SUMMARY
Preparing to Leave Sinai 1:1 to 9:23
Departure from Sinai 10:1-36
Complaints 11;1 to 12:16
Border of the Promised Land 13:1 to 14:45
Wandering in the Wilderness 15:1 to 27:11
Preparing to Enter Again 27:12 to 36:13

PREPARING TO LEAVE MT SINAI

1:1-54 **The First Census** On the first day of the second month of the second year the LORD told Moses to count the people as they prepared to leave Sinai for the Promised Land. Eleven tribes were included. The tribe of Levi was not counted as they were specially dedicated to the LORD and responsible for the Tabernacle. The two sons of Joseph, Ephraim and Manasseh were included in their place. The total number of men came to 603,550.

The people took great care to preserve their ancestry 1:17-19 from Adam down to the birth of the Messiah Jesus Christ Lk 3:23-37.

Arrangement of the Camps

2:1-34 **The Tribal Camps** were arranged in order around the Tabernacle which faced east, toward the sunrise. The Levites encircled the Tabernacle – Moses and Aaron camped in front, to the east 3:38. This was also to be the marching order.

3:1-39 **The Levites counted** – separated for special duties.

3:11-13 The firstborn son of each family was set aside when the LORD struck down the firstborn of Egypt. They would be released (redeemed) by replacement with the Levites who would serve before the LORD at the Tabernacle.

3:40-47 **The firstborn counted** – set aside to be redeemed.

4:1-49 **The duties of the Levites** Aaron, his sons and family as priests were responsible for the duties of the Tabernacle. Strict instructions were given for the care and transport of all holy items.

4:1-20 The Kohathites cared for the items of the Tabernacle.

4:21-28 The Gershonites cared for the Tabernacle & Courtyard.

4:29-33 The Merarites cared for the structure of the Tabernacle.

4:34-49 Each Levite had his work assigned to him.

The Holiness of God The great attention to the care of the Tabernacle and Court was required to emphasize the holy nature of God 4:4,16,20. We must show this same reverence, awe and respect *for our God is a consuming fire Heb 12:28,29*.

5:1-31 **Purity in the Camp** – moral purity and hygiene was required.

6:1-21 **The Vow of a Nazirite** – one set apart for the LORD.

6:22-27 The LORD bless you and keep you; the LORD make his face shine upon you and be gracious to you; the LORD turn his face toward you and give you peace v24-26. We can bless others this way – we are the children of the blessing. A silver scroll of this text was found in Jerusalem from 7th century BC confirming its early date.

7:1-89 **Dedication of the Tabernacle** – gifts were willingly given.

8:1-26 **Consecration of the Levites** – set apart for the worship, service, care and transport of the Tabernacle.

Celebrating the Second Passover

9:1-14 Twelve months after leaving Egypt they celebrated Passover.

The Presence of the LORD

9:15-23 **On completion of the Tabernacle** the pillar representing the Presence of the LORD covered it – as a cloud by day and fire by night Ex 13:20-22. The people were led by the cloud across the trackless wilderness - if the cloud remained they stayed, if the cloud lifted they set out.

As the people had prepared themselves to embrace the Presence of the LORD in the same way we can learn to abide, dwell, walk with the LORD and be led by the Holy Spirit Jn 15:1-8; Gal 5:25; Rev 3:20.

DEPARTURE FROM MT SINAI

10:1-10 Trumpets were used to call the people when to assemble.

10:11-13 On the twentieth day of the second month of the second year the cloud lifted and the people moved from Mt Sinai.

The Journey so far They had left Egypt on the fifteenth day of the first month of the first (new) year Ex 12:1 and arrived at Mt Sinai on the first day of the third month – a journey of six weeks Ex 19:1. They remained at Sinai for eleven and half months. As they departed now this was the first time Israel had marched as a nation and they set out north for the Promised Land v13.

10:14-32 They marched in order – Judah, Issachar and Zebulun, then the Tabernacle. Ruben, Simeon and Gad followed by the Kohathites with the Ark and holy things, then Ephraim and Manasseh, Benjamin, Dan, Asher and Naphtali. Before they arrived at a location the Tabernacle was to be set up first v21.

Hobab, brother-in-law of Moses was requested to stay for his knowledge of the desert. Reuel, father-in-law of Moses v29; Ex 2:18 was also called Jethro Ex 18:1.

10:33-36 There was great joy as they set out under the direction of God. We will know this joy as we are led daily by the Holy Spirit Mk 16:20.

Exodus Chronology – Journey from Egypt to the Promised Land

Event	reference	duration	Out of Egypt
Departed Egypt	Ex 12:1		
Arrived at Sinai	Ex 19:1	6 weeks	6 weeks
Tabernacle completed	Ex 40:17	10 months	11.5 months
Departed Sinai	Nu 10:11	6 weeks	13 months
Arrived at Kadesh	De 1:1,2	11 days	
Spies view the Promised Land	Nu 13:2	40 days	15 months
Return to the Wilderness	Nu 14:45		
Wandering - Kadesh to Moab	De 1:3; 2:1	38.75 years	
Time from Egypt to Moab			40 years

COMPLAINTS

11:1-17 The people complained about their hardships Former slaves, now a chosen people belonging to God and they were complaining again – they received a warning from God. We must be thankful *in all circumstances 1Thes 5:18,19.* They were provided daily with manna but wanted more Ex 16:11-14, 31. The complaints of the people troubled Moses v10.

The LORD instructed Moses to separate out the seventy leaders. He would place his Holy Spirit on them v16,17; Ex 18:21; 24:1. It is important that leaders and elders be appointed for their spiritual walk as well as their abilities Acts 6:3-5.

11:18-23 Is the LORD's arm too short? The complaints of the people even caused Moses to doubt – the impact of discord.

Joshua was the aid of Moses v28.

11:24-30 **The Spirit on the Leaders** The infilling of the Holy Spirit is vital for all those in leadership and service roles. Moses longed that all God's people might be committed and filled with the Holy Spirit v29. This infilling is available to all who respond to Jesus as Savior and LORD in humility and commitment Acts 2:4.

11:31-35 The LORD provided quail for a second time Ex 16:13.

Leadership Challenged

12:1,2 Miriam and Aaron began to talk against Moses It is not good to talk against the leadership – they are the LORD's anointed.

12:3 Moses was more humble than anyone else God respects and honors humility - it demonstrates dependence on God 1Sam 24:5-7; 26:8-11; Is 57:15; Jas 4:6. Jesus *humbled himself Phil 2:8.* How do you make a prince humble – assign him to the desert for forty years! Ex 3:1.

12:4-8 With him I speak face to face v8 The aim of each person should be to come into relationship with the Creator. The possibility of intimacy with God is the goal of life. This is now made possible by the new and living way opened for us through Jesus Heb 10:19-22. The expression 'face to face' is a metaphor for openness. God has no visible form Deu 4:15.

12:9-16 **The LORD defends his chosen servants** The punishment of Miriam was severe and shows the importance to God of authority.

THE BORDER OF THE PROMISED LAND – opportunity to enter!

13:1-25 **Twelve spies were sent out** at God's request as a further test of the faith of the people. They would see the conditions - the prosperity of the land and the magnitude of the task. Would they trust God to fulfill his promises?

They had come from Mt Sinai to Kadesh-Barnea in the Desert of Paran, on the southern border of Canaan, a journey of 11 days Deu 1:1,2. The spies traveled 140 km north reaching Hebron and even to Jerusalem. They returned after 40 days with abundant produce v23.

The REPORT - two conclusions

13:26,27 **The Good Report** *It does flow with milk and honey* This was the common observation of all the spies and confirmed what God had promised Ex 3:8,17. All God's promises are true and are fulfilled in Jesus 2Cor 1:20.

13:28-33 **The Conclusion** The same circumstances were viewed by the twelve spies – the same evidence. There were two perceptions from the same information.

- **A Pessimistic Outlook** Ten of the spies gave **a negative view based on circumstances** – they feared the inhabitants of the land v28,29 - they saw through the eyes of doubt and self ability
- **An Optimistic Outlook** Caleb encouraged the people with **a positive view based on faith in God's promises** – *we can certainly do it v30* - Caleb and Joshua saw through the eyes of faith.

The Grounds for Doubt *We seemed like grasshoppers in our own eyes and we looked the same to them v33.* This observation was not rational - they magnified their fears and exaggerated the task.

The Grounds for Faith We must not look at things based on our own limitations. We need to see things based on the promises in God's Word and on what God is able to do with us and through us when we put our trust in him – *he is able to do immeasurably more than all we ask or imagine, according to his power that is at work within us Eph 3:20.*

The People Rebelled

14:1-5 The people chose to believe the pessimistic opinion - it is usually the most comfortable - rather than step out with faith in God they grumbled. The same choice lies before us today – to choose God or the world.

14:6-9 **Further Grounds for Faith** Our faith must be based on knowledge - it must have a foundation. Joshua and Caleb knew God - who he is and what he had done in the past - they also knew what he had promised -

- *If the LORD is pleased with us – we will swallow them up v8* What confidence we can have in our God! Faith is taking action that includes God
- *Their protection is gone, but the LORD is with us v9* We need to include the spiritual dimension in our daily walk both in our perception and in our decisions 2Kin 6;16,17.

The Glory of the LORD Appeared

14:10-12 How long will these people treat me with contempt The great sin of mankind is to deny God. Then comes the sin of doubting that he cares or that he will be true to his promises. Despite all the evidence of God's provision – the plagues, crossing the Red Sea, provision in the wilderness, the encounter at Mt Sinai – the people still would not put their faith and trust in God. They would prefer to live within their own limitations.

14:13-19 **Moses Pleaded with God** - for forty days Deu 9:25. The appeal for mercy was on the basis of God's strength, his character and his love. It was this strength, character and love that sent Jesus to the cross so that we might be forgiven our sins v19.

14:20-39 **Consequences of Unbelief** Pardon was granted but there were consequences – *who disobeyed me and tested me ten times v22.* There was a history of complaints –

Event	ref	Event	ref
1. Crossing the Red Sea	Ex 14:11	6. The Golden Calf	Ex 32:1
2. Bitter Waters of Marah	Ex 15:24	7. Hardships	Nu 11:1
3. Food, manna & quail	Ex 16:2	8. Food	Nu 11:4
4. Water from the rock	Ex 17:2	9. Aaron's revolt	Nu 12:1
5. At Mt Sinai	Ex 20:19	10. Entering the Land	Nu 14:22

No one who has treated me with contempt will ever see the Promised Land v23. Many people treat God with contempt today. They deny him, ignore him, blame him and profane his name - they have a self-righteousness that regards themselves as acceptable to God. They perceive God as made in their own image and determine how he should act – to please them. Continued rejection of God will result in his rejection of you – *the wages of sin is death, but the gift of God is eternal life through Jesus Christ our Lord Rom 6:23.*

Those who honor God will in turn be honored v24,30.

Caleb and Joshua would possess the Promised Land – after a 39 year wait! It is a sign of greatness that they did not waver from their commitment because of the delay - both were faithful to the end -

• **As for me and my house we will serve the LORD** These were Joshua's parting words Jos 24:15

• **Give me this mountain** Forty-five years later Caleb chose for his inheritance the very location that the spies had feared (Anakites in the hill country) - it was still to be conquered 13:22,33; Jos 14:12,13.

14:40-45 **The day of opportunity was over** - *nevertheless, in their presumption they went up towards the high hill country v44* They acted on their own initiative in desperation and regret but it was too late. The people who could have possessed the land but did not want to were now driven back - the Presence of the LORD made the difference Ps 127:1-2; Zec 4:6-9. The Amalekites whom they previously defeated under Joshua and Moses were now their conquerors. They had not learned the lesson of trusting

God and commitment to prayer Ex 17:8-15. We must respond to the LORD when he speaks and always go in his strength – *trust in the Lord with all your heart and do not rely on your own understanding; in all your ways acknowledge him and he will direct your paths Pro 3:5-8.*
Israel would eventually destroy the Amalekites. However again independence and disobedience would be their downfall 1Sam 15:2-8, 20-23.

A Positive Outlook to Life - If God be for us Rom 8:31
We can learn important guidelines from these events -

• Develop a positive attitude - thoughts multiply for good and bad, both positive and negative - in so doing you will have the best chance of success
• Be confident of God's promises - this requires knowing the Word of God and putting it into action in your activities Jos 1:8,9
• Believe in what you are doing - work out your mission and vision with God - rather than asking God to help you in what you are doing, get involved in what God is doing
• Believe in your own ability - see yourself from God's perspective – the LORD is with us 14:9
• See problems and difficulties as opportunities to be addressed - instead of barriers they are really steps in the plan 13:30
• Do not be anxious - what does worry add? Cancel negative thoughts, feelings and talk with positive thoughts and actions Mt 6:25,31-34; Jn 14:27
• Be prepared for the battle, to put in the effort required - success is part inspiration, mostly hard work
• Be proactive - make plans, set objectives, review progress and always act on the opportunities God gives through the leading of the Holy Spirit
• Learn from every experience, good & bad – there is a purpose
• Love everyone, exclude no one and move with the movers
• Never give up – be task oriented – the result is what counts - our feelings may vary but not our drive 2Cor 4:16-18
• Develop your relationship with God - he is the foundation for our confidence and the basis for our faith Ps 89:15-18; Rom 15:13.

WANDERING IN THE WILDERNESS
The people were defeated and spent the next thirty-nine years in the wilderness until all those over 20 years of age had died v32-35; Deu

1:35,36. They had complained that Moses brought them out into the wilderness to die Ex 14:11. Now, because of their lack of faith that was what would happen. The sad lesson of this failure is that the people lost the chance to enter the Promised Land and to reach their potential because they would not put their trust in God.

They failed to enter God's rest Ps 95:7-11 We must respond to God today while it is the day of grace. There is a rest for the people of God Heb 4:1-11 - we can enter that rest as we walk in faith and learn to trust God's promises and guidance. There is confidence in life & eternal assurance Mt 11:28-30.

Wilderness location Hormah was near Kadesh. For many years the people made their way around the wilderness hill country of Seir, south of Edom until the LORD gave them directions to return north in preparation to again approach the land of promise 33:1-56; Deu 2:1,14; Jos 3:1 (ref p91-93).

15:1-41 **Review of Offerings and Duties** Lev 1:1 to 7:38 *Offerings made by fire – as an aroma pleasing to the LORD* This explains a reason for the burnt offerings. External garments reminded the people of their chosen status v37. When we read the Word of God regularly we have it written in our hearts to keep us from sin and to encourage us to attempt great things.

Leadership Again Challenged

16:1-50 Three Levite men together with 250 community leaders challenged Moses. He fell on his face for he knew the consequences. The LORD would resolve the dispute. *It is against the LORD that you have banded together v11.* The LORD appoints and anoints leadership Dan 2:21; 4:17. The challengers showed their contempt by misquoting Moses v14. Discontent breeds rashness. The LORD threatened to judge the whole community v21.

Moses appealed again to God's mercy - *God of the spirits of all mankind v22* - all people and nations belong to God and will be accountable to him. The people were required to separate from the wrongdoers v24. The ground swallowed the challengers and a plague killed those who continued to oppose Moses v31.

Leadership Confirmed – Aaron's staff budded

17:1-12 It is not good to leave leadership issues unresolved. Each of the twelve tribal leaders put their staff inside the Tabernacle – overnight Aaron's staff sprouted, budded, blossomed and produced almonds, clearly confirming his leadership of the priesthood. His staff was kept in the Tabernacle as a reminder against further rebellion.

18:1-32 The duties and privileges of the priesthood and the rest of the Levites were confirmed v1. They also received part of the offerings and the tithe in return for their duties at the Tabernacle.

19:1-22 Purifying water was specially prepared for cleansing.

Moses' Anger – water from the rock

20:1-13 After the death of Miriam the people complained again for lack of water. Moses inquired of the LORD – he was told to take his staff and speak to a certain rock which would bring forth water - a further test! Moses struck the rock twice claiming his own ability to meet the need of the people v9. Because of this act of disrespect he was denied entrance to the Promised Land – recall Ex 17:2-7. The responsibility of leadership for obedience, trust and to honor God is great. Always remember the work is the LORD's – it is his kingdom, his power and glory.
We can also learn from this that feelings must be contained.

20:14-21 **Israel denied passage by Edom** Located south of the Dead Sea the people of Edom were descendants of Lot and remained antagonistic to Israel throughout the kingdom period. Israel was told not to disturb Edom or Moab Deu 2:4-6, 8,9. We must avoid conflict with brethren Ps 133.

20:22-29 **Death of Aaron** The people left Kadesh and came to Mt Hor at the border of Edom where Aaron died v24. He was succeeded as high priest by his son Eleazar.

Beginning of the Conquest

21:1-3 **The defeat of the Canaanite king of Arad** marked the start of the conquest of the Promised Land. These were possibly the same people who drove the Israelites back from their abortive attempt to enter Canaan thirty-nine years before 14:45.

The Bronze Snake

21:4-9 The people grew impatient – again they complained against God. Venomous snakes attacked them. A bronze snake was made – *anyone who was bitten and looked at the snake lived* - an act of faith and obedience v9. This event is significant because Jesus referred to it as confirmation of the power of his impending death to forgive sin – *just as Moses lifted up the snake in the desert, so the Son of Man must be lifted up, that everyone who believes in him may have eternal life Jn 3:14,15.*

The Journey to Moab

21:10-35 The people moved north skirting around the borders of Edom and then Moab to the Arnon River to approach Canaan from the east v13. They fought against the Amorite kings of Sihon and Og who lived north of Moab and defeated them v21 taking possession of their first land v31,35.

Conflict with Moab – Balak, Balaam and the donkey

22:1-41 The Israelites were now camped at the Jordan River on the Plains of Moab across from Jericho v1. Moabites were descendants of Lot and were in fear of Israel, now on their border. Balak, king of Moab sent to Balaam, a prophet on the Euphrates River to obtain protection from the Israelites. Balaam had respect for the Hebrew God who has power over all mankind. Balaam consulted God and was told not to go because Israel was a blessed people v12. A second delegation offered a handsome reward v15 – even so Balaam could *not go beyond the command of the LORD my God v18.*

This showed his reverence for God. His second request to God revealed that he was tempted by the reward. He was told to go *but do only what I tell you v20.* We must not be tempted to press God's favor for worldly gains. On the way Balaam was challenged by an angel but was too consumed by his greed to notice. The donkey was used to warn him of the serious nature of his actions v21-34. He confirmed to Balak – *I must speak only what God puts in my mouth v38.*

God's Protection of His People – five prophetic words

23:1-12 **The first prophetic word** - Balaam acknowledged the blessing on Israel - *how can I curse those whom God has not cursed?* God's people cannot be cursed! They are a people who live apart - under the blessing v9.

23:13-26 **The second prophetic word** - the character of God is revealed – he does not change and will not go back on his Word - it cannot be reversed v19. *I have received command to bless; God has blessed and I cannot change it v20.* We are freed from the curse of the world and no one can bring a curse against us – *Christ redeemed us from* *the curse of the law by becoming a curse for us – that the blessing given to Abraham might come to the Gentiles Gal 3:13,14. **There is no sorcery against Jacob, no divination against Israel v23.*** This promise applies as well to those who are in Christ.

It also confirms that we must not be involved in the occult Lev 19:31.

23:27 to 24:14* The third prophetic word** - although Balaam was not totally committed he revered God and acknowledged his authority. ***May those who bless you be blessed and those who curse you be cursed v9 – this promise still applies to the believer.

***24:15-19* The fourth prophetic word** - *I see him, but not now: I behold him, but not near. A star will come out of Jacob; a scepter will rise out of Israel* – this amazing prophecy foretold of David as king of Israel and ultimately of the coming of Jesus as Messiah v17; Is 9:7.

***24:20-25* The fifth prophetic word** - Israel will have future victory over the surrounding nations. Balaam departed without his reward – Balak returned with a curse on Moab.

Israel Seduced by Moab

25:1-18 While Israel camped on the border of Moab some became involved with the women of Shittim Jos 3:1. They then joined in the worship of idols. This strategy was suggested to Moab by Balaam 31:16. What Moab could not achieve by curses they achieved by tempting the weakness of the Israelites. We must learn the dangers of close association with the people and ways of the world. Judgment was swift and required separation. Phinehas, son of Eleazer the high priest was rewarded for his zeal v10-13.

The Second Census

26:1-51 All those over 20 years of age at the time of the first attempt to enter the Promised Land had died in the wilderness except for Moses, Joshua and Caleb. A census of the new generation of men came to 601,730.

26:52-65 The land in Canaan was assigned by tribe and number.

27:1-11 The inheritance of land to daughters was provided.

Joshua appointed to succeed Moses

***27:12-17* Moses was led by the LORD** He ascended Mt Nebo overlooking Canaan – he would see the land but not enter it. He showed his greatness as a leader by asking the LORD to appoint his successor v15-17.

27:18-23 **Joshua's Credentials** Born in Egypt of the tribe of Ephram, a slave for some 40 years he became personal aid and assistant of Moses. He led Israel in their first battle against the Amalekites on the way to Mt Sinai Ex 17:8-16. He accompanied Moses onto Mt Sinai to receive the Ten Commandments and attended the Tent of Meeting lingering in the Presence after Moses had left Ex 24:13; 33:11. One of the twelve spies sent to view the Promised Land he gave a favorable report and was permitted to enter the land after the forty years wandering Nu 13:8; 14:6,30. He was filled with the Holy Spirit and wisdom after being anointed by Moses Deu 34:9. A man of discipline and courage he had the respect of the Israelites as they gained entry to the Promised Land and throughout his life Jos 24:31. Joshua was commissioned by Moses v23.

Review of Feasts, Festivals and Offerings

28:1 to 30:16 The form of worship, appointed feasts and offerings were reviewed for the new generation -

- Daily offerings – morning and twilight 28:1-8; Lev 1:1 to 7:38
- Sabbath offering 28:9,10; Lev 23:3; Monthly offerings 28:11-15
- Passover and Feast of Unleavened Bread 28:16-25; Lev 23:4-14
- Feast of Weeks (Pentecost) 28:26-31; Lev 23:15-22
- Feast of Trumpets 29:1-6; Lev 23:23-25
- Day of Atonement 29:7-11; Lev 16:1-34; 23:26-32
- Feast of Tabernacles 29:12-40; Lev 23:33-44
- Vows and family relationships 30:1-16.

31:1-54 **Vengeance against Midian** They were nomads who inhabited the southern desert in the region of Moab and were complicit in the deception of Israel 22:4; 25:1. The LORD commanded vengeance be taken to cleanse his people v2. Balaam was also killed – he must have remained in Moab. His advice had caused the Israelites to become involved in idol worship v8,16.

32:1-42 **Settlement East of Jordan** Some of the people saw the land on the east side of the Jordan River was good so they made a request to settle there as their inheritance. Moses made them agree to cross the Jordan and assist the remaining tribes to gain their inheritances. He then assigned to the tribes of Gad, Reuben and half tribe of Manasseh the land east of Jordan.

REVIEW OF THE JOURNEY OF ISRAEL

***33:1-49* Review of the Journey** Moses was commanded to record (write) the stages of the journey from coming out of Egypt to the present day for future history v2. Reference was made to Mt Sinai v15 but not to Kadesh Barnea 32:8. They were now on the east side of the Jordan River ready to cross into the land of promise near Beth Jesimoth and Abel Shittim v48,49; 25:1; Jos 3:1.

33:50-56 The LORD instructed the people to drive out the inhabitants of Canaan and take possession of the land. They were to destroy all their idols and high places of worship. Opportunity had been given to the inhabitants to turn from evil - now their sin had reached full measure Gen 15:16. If Israel allowed them to stay they would adopt their evil ways and they too would be judged v55,56. This is in fact what happened in the divided kingdoms - *they mocked God's messengers, despised his words and scoffed at his prophets until the wrath of the LORD was aroused against his people and there was no remedy 2Chr 36:15,16.* This is a warning for all generations Deu 7:1-26; 1Cor 10:11.

Allocation of the Boundaries in Canaan

34:1-29 A leader was appointed from each tribe to assign the land as an inheritance by lot and by number of people.

***35:1-34* The Levites** were allocated towns to live in from each area assigned to the tribes. This meant that the priests would be located throughout the land to provide instruction, counseling and motivation. Six of these towns would be 'Cities of Refuge' to allow security for accused people until proven guilty (the rule of presumption of innocence).

36:1-13 Details for the inheritance for daughters were also defined.

Conclusion - Israel recommitted to the Covenant and had come to the end of their wandering in the wilderness. They were now prepared and poised on the border of Canaan ready once more to cross over into the land of promise.

Deuteronomy – 'the second law'

Introduction – The people of Israel spent thirty-nine years in the wilderness until all those over 20 years of age at the time of the first attempt to enter the Promised Land had died. Moses gave three farewell addresses to the new generation as they prepared to enter the land under the leadership of Joshua. They had not experienced the giving of the Law on Mt Sinai or the failure of the previous attempt.

He reminded them of all that God had done for them, reviewed the Law and Festivals and reconfirmed God's Covenant with them.

Author – Written by Moses 31:9,24; Num 33:2; Neh 13:1.

Period – The week before Israel finally entered the Promised Land.

Theme – Review of the Law The previous generation received the Law at Mt Sinai but failed to enter the land due to lack of faith. Now the new generation was poised to enter and they needed to be reminded of the importance of a right relationship with God.

There are over 80 quotations from Deuteronomy in the New Testament.

SUMMARY
Moses' First Address – Review of God's Faithfulness 1:1 to 4:49
Moses' Second Address – Review of the Law 5;1 to 26:19
Moses' Third Address – Terms of the Covenant 27:1-30
Offer of Life and Prosperity or Death and Separation 30:11-20
Joshua Succeeded Moses 31:1-23
The Book of the Law 31:24 to 34:12

MOSES' FIRST ADDRESS – Review of God's faithfulness
1:1-5 **East of Jordan** Israel camped on the northern border of Moab, east of the Jordan River, the final location before entering the land promised to Abraham Gen 12:1; 17:8; Num 22:1; 26:3 – forty years after they left Egypt.

1:6-46 **The Journey So Far** Moses recalled the route from Horeb (Mt Sinai) to Kadesh Barnea and the sending out of the twelve spies v19, the refusal to enter the land and their relegation to the wilderness v46. God treats us as his children when we put our trust in him v31.

2:1 to 3:11 **Wandering** They remained in the southern hill country of Seir, near Kadesh and south of Edom until all those over 20 years of age had died 2:14,15. Then the LORD gave them directions to return northeast in preparation for again approaching the Promised Land 2:1,2. They were instructed to avoid conflict with Edom, descendants of Esau v4 and with Moab and the Ammonites, descendants of Lot v9. They defeated two Amorite kings gaining possession of their first land 2:24; 3:1; Num 21:21-31.

3:12-29 **Land East of Jordan was Assigned** Moses was not permitted to enter v26. Joshua was appointed the new leader v28. The valley of Beth Peor was on the plains of Moab v29; Num 33:49; Jos 3:1.

4:1-14 **Obedience Required** The people were reminded that the promises of God's Covenant included the condition of obedience to his commands. *The LORD our God is near us whenever we pray to him v7.* This is the assurance we have in God as reinforced by Jesus Mt 18:20. The Ten Commandments are not only sound principles v8 but are the basis for our way of life as summarized by Jesus – *love the LORD your God with all your heart and soul and mind and strength and love your neighbor as yourself Mk 12:30,31.*

4:15-20 God is unique Spirit – so worship of idols or putting anything before God is forbidden v15-20.

4:21-24 **The Holiness of God** The character of God requires absolute commitment – we must not be half-hearted towards God – *the LORD your God is a consuming fire, a jealous God v24*; Heb 12:28,29.

4:25-31 **Failure Foretold** Moses predicted the failure of Israel as a nation. It was not possible for human nature to achieve the standard of God but this had to be demonstrated. The northern kingdom would be scattered v27 and the southern kingdom exiled – only a remnant would be saved. It was necessary that a new spirit be put into mankind – this was made possible by the coming of the Lord Jesus Christ Ezk 36:26,27; Jn 14:26.

If you seek the LORD your God you will find him if you look for him with all your heart and soul v29 – when we are serious about knowing God he will reveal himself to us, regardless of our past Jer 29:13; 33:3.

4:32-40 **The Glory of God and His Invitation** The greatest decision each one must make in life is to acknowledge God and commit to know him – *acknowledge and take to heart this day that the LORD is God in heaven above and on the earth below – there is no other v39.*

4:41-49 The cities of refuge were identified.

MOSES' SECOND ADDRESS – Review of the Law

5:1-33 The Ten Commandments were reviewed Ex 20:1-21.

6:1-25 **The LORD our God is one LORD** Love the LORD with all your heart, soul, mind and strength v5. This 'Shema' is the defining statement of the Jewish faith, stated twice each day - confirmed by Jesus as the greatest commandment Mk 12:29-31.

If we obey all this law – that will be our righteousness v25. Now a second righteousness is revealed through Jesus – *by faith from first to last Rom 1:17; 3:22.*

7:1-26 **You are a holy people** They were commanded to destroy the nations of Canaan and their idols. *You must destroy them totally v2.* Israel was used to bring judgment on the nations of Canaan for their idolatry and corrupt ways. Every idol and person had to be destroyed so that Israel would not be led to follow the evil practices 4:15-20,23,24; Nu 33:50-56. The sad fact is that they did adopt the evil practices of the nations that were not removed 2Chr 33:9.

We are a holy people chosen by God as his treasured possession v6; Ex 19:5,6; 1Pet 2:9,10. Obedience brings blessing in all areas of life – family, produce, prosperity, health v13-15. Victory is given by the LORD – so we must remove all things that are detestable to God to remain separate from the world v25; Mt 5:48. Temptation and wrongdoing often result from bad associations.

8:1-20 **Remain faithful to God** He will test us to reveal our hearts and keep us humble so *we will live on every Word that comes from the mouth of the LORD! v3.* When things go well remember it is because of God's provision and goodness – *it is he who gives you the ability to produce wealth and so confirms his Covenant v18.*

9:1-29 **It is God who goes with us** Not because of our righteousness but because of his purpose and mercy. Three times Moses spent forty days before the LORD – to receive the Law 9:9; Ex 31:18; 32:1; to ask forgiveness for the calf idol 9:18;10:10; Ex 32:19,31 and to ask forgiveness when the people refused to go into the Promised Land 9:25; Num 14:11.

10:1-22 **The Two Tablets** containing the Ten Commandments were remade and placed in the Ark representing God's Presence with the people Ex 34:1. It was now up to the people. *What does the LORD ask of you but to fear him, walk in his ways, love him and serve him v12;* Mic 6:8.

The nature of God was reviewed – he owns the heavens yet sets his affection on his people v14,15. He is *God of gods and LORD of lords, the great God, mighty and awesome v17.*
He is your praise; he is your God v21.

11:1-32 **The Response of the People** As a result of the goodness of God the manner of life for the people must be to love him and keep his requirements. They must fix his words in their hearts and minds and teach them to their children v18. There is a blessing for those who obey and a curse for those who do not v26-28.

12:1-32 **The Place and Manner of Worship** A number of locations were set aside for worship including Gilgal Jos 4:20; Gibeon 1Kin 3:4; Shiloh Jos 19:51 and finally Jerusalem 1Kin 6:1. However the place of blessing is not in a building or location but living in the Presence of the LORD v7 – made possible now by Jesus Jn 14:17; Gal 5:25.

13:1-18 Remain faithful to God – purge evil from among you.

14:1-29 Acceptable food and tithes.

15:1-23 Kindness to the poor and the year of cancelling debts.

16:1-21 Passover and Feasts; Justice; Rejection of false gods.

17:1-13 Law Courts and justice.

17:14-20 **Rules for Kings** The future desire for a king was foretold and guidelines were given –
• a king must avoid excesses (wealth and horses from Egypt) v16
• he would need to avoid many wives v17
• he would have to follow carefully the Word of God - he would be required to write out the Law, keep it with him, read it daily and apply it so that he would revere the LORD.
It is notable that the future kings did not follow these rules, particularly Solomon who lost 10 tribes of the kingdom within a week of his death 1Kin 11:1-13.
The instructions concerning the importance of the Word of God and the reasons for regular reading are relevant today for every believer.

18:1-8 Offerings of Priests and Levites

18:9-14 **Avoiding the Occult** Involvement in any spiritual practice where God is not the center is to be completely avoided. In these matters we must be blameless v13. Many have failed by their 'harmless interest', not realizing the offence to God.

18:15-22 **The Promise of the Messiah** *The LORD your God will raise a prophet like you v18.*

- As the people needed Moses to give them God's Word so in the future God would raise a leader who would complete God's plan –
- He would be known by the fulfillment of his words – this promise was fulfilled in Jesus Christ
- Like Moses, Jesus came to deliver his people from their bondage and bring them to God to worship him
- Like Moses, Jesus also performed amazing miracles to confirm the truth of his ministry
- Moses was faithful as a servant in God's house testifying to what would be said in the future – he was a member of God's house
- Jesus has greater honor because he is a Son over God's house Heb 3:2-6 – he is the Head of the church Eph 4:15,16
- Moses was not able to keep the people from sin
- Jesus delivers from the penalty and the power of sin and gives eternal life to those who believe in him Rom 6:23; Heb 9:26-28.

More instructions reviewed

19:1-21 Guidelines for Cities of Refuge and Witnesses.

20:1-20 **Rules for war** When we are called by God to undertake a task we must remember it is the LORD who fights for us to give us the victory v4. We need to make up our minds to commit and then not be faint-hearted.

21:1-22 Unsolved murder v1; captives v10; right of firstborn v15; a rebellious son v18.

21:22-23 **The Curse of Execution** - Jesus bore the curse of our sins for us on Calvary Gal 3:13-14.

22:1 to 25:19 Sundry Social Laws

26:1-15 **Firstfruits and Tithes** Offer to the LORD the firstfruits of your provision.

26:16-19 **The Result of Obedience to the LORD** will be blessing, provision and prosperity in his service.

MOSES' THIRD ADDRESS – Terms of the covenant

27:1-26 **The Covenant Renewal** The Covenant was broken at Kadesh thirty-nine years before and would have to be renewed in the Promised Land Num 14:30. The people were instructed to meet at the twin mountains of Ebal and Gerizim near Shechem (the future Samaria). They must set up an altar – half the people assembled on each mountain and the Law would be read by the Levites – the curses from Ebal, the blessings from Gerizim – the people would confirm their acceptance. This took place under Joshua Jos 8;30.

28:1-14 **Blessings for Obedience** Consider what Israel might have been if they had continued to be faithful to God and his Word.
These blessings are foreseen in the millennium age Is 60:1-22; Jer 31:1-9; Zec 14:1-16; Rom 11:25-32; Rev 20:4-6.
The blessings of God are available in the Christian era 2Cor 1:20.

28:15-68 **Curses for Disobedience** Consider the suffering of Israel under Rome AD 70 v47-50 and in the 1940's v63-67.

29:1-29 **The Covenant Conditions Emphasized** They were reminded of God's faithfulness in meeting their needs.

30:1-10 If they turned away from God and then repented he would restore them.

OFFER OF LIFE and PROSPERITY or DEATH and SEPERATION

30:11-20 **The LORD is Your Life** v19,20 The conclusion of the three addresses by Moses was based on the character of God and applies equally today. If we acknowledge God and seek to walk in his ways we will receive blessing in all areas of our lives Mt 6:33. We have the Word of God available to us today – to believe it and obey brings life – to deny it leads to separation from God both now and for eternity v14; Rom 6:23; 10:8-10.

JOSHUA SUCCEEDED MOSES

31:1-14 Moses was now 120 years old. Joshua became the new leader Num 27:18.

31:15-23 **Future Rebellion** Future failure of the people in the Promised Land was again predicted and God's provision for repentance proclaimed. We know the weakness of the human heart and will. We can be thankful for God's mercy available to us through the death of Jesus – *if we claim to be without sin we deceive ourselves and the truth is not in us. If we confess our sins, he is faithful and just and will forgive us our sins and purify us from all unrighteousness 1Jn 1:8, 9.*
Success for obedience was promised v23.

THE BOOK OF THE LAW

31:24-26 Moses finished writing down in a book the words of this law from beginning to end – this is the internal evidence that Moses was the author of the first five Books of the Bible. Trained as a prince of Egypt he had the necessary skills. Archeology confirms writing in Egypt and Sinai before 1440 BC. Jesus confirmed both the person of Moses and his writing skills – *he wrote about me! Jn 5:46.*

It is a miracle that we have these writing available to us today to guide us in our daily life.

Song of Moses about God's Greatness These words are your life

32:1-52 **The Greatness of God** Moses testified from his experience to the character of God – his works are perfect, his ways are just, he does no wrong, he is faithful and upright Ex 15:1-21. It cannot be denied that *he is your Father, your Creator, who made you and formed you v6.* It is of great assurance for those who know him to understand that *he guards you as the apple of his eye v10.* God has to stir us like baby eagles from our comfort zones to develop our characters and become effective in service v11.

God is Sovereign - in complete control of every circumstance.

It is mine to avenge; I will repay. This relieves us from the burden and the need to get even v35-39.

33:1-29 **Moses' Blessing** *The eternal God is your refuge and underneath are the everlasting arms.* A promise confirmed by Jesus and experienced by all who put their trust in him v27; Jn 10:28.

34:1-12 **Death of Moses** He climbed Mt Nebo from the plains of Moab to the top of Pisgah, across from Jericho – there he died v5.

Moses is remembered as the greatest of prophets because of his relationship with God and for the tremendous work he was called to undertake v10.

Conclusion - After forty years of wandering, the people under Joshua would finally enter the Promised Land.

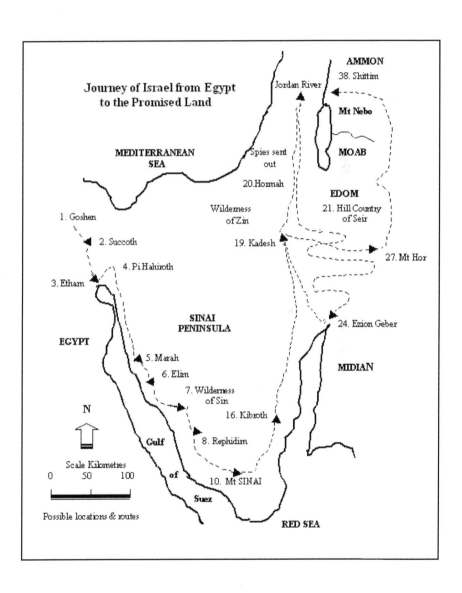

Journey of Israel from Egypt
to the Promised Land

AMMON
38. Shittim

Jordan River

Mt Nebo

MEDITERRANEAN
SEA

Spies sent
out

MOAB

20. Hormah

EDOM

Wilderness
of Zin

21. Hill Country
of Seir

1. Goshen

19. Kadesh

2. Succoth

27. Mt Hor

4. Pi Hahiroth

3. Etham

SINAI
PENINSULA

24. Ezion Geber

EGYPT

5. Marah

MIDIAN

6. Elim

7. Wilderness
of Sin

N

16. Kibroth

8. Rephidim

Gulf

Scale Kilometres

0   50   100

of

10. Mt SINAI

Suez

Possible locations & routes

RED SEA

Journey of Israel to the Promised Land

	Event	location	duration	Out of Egypt	date	ref 1	ref 2
1	**Departed Egypt** - First Passover	Goshen	1 day		14/1/'1	Ex 12:1	Nu 33:3
2	First Camp - Firstborn Consecrated	Succoth			15/1/'1	Ex 13:20	Nu 33:5
3	Second Camp - Edge of Wilderness	Etham				Ex 13:20	Nu 33:6
4	**Red Sea Crossing** - Egypt's Defeat	Pi Hahiroth				Ex 14:2	Nu 33:8
5	Bitter Water - Wilderness of Shur	Marah				Ex 15:22	Nu 33:8
6	Oasis - Wilderness of Shur	Elim				Ex 15:27	Nu 33:9
7	Manna & Quail - Wliderness of Sin					Ex 16:1	Nu 33:11
8	Water from the Rock - South Sinai	Rephidim				Ex 17:1	Nu 33:14
9	Amalekites Defeated - Moses' Prayer	Rephidim				Ex 17:8	
10	**Ten Commandments**	Mount Sinai	6 weeks	6 weeks	1/3/'1	Ex 19:1	Nu 33:15
11	Tabernacle Set Up, Dedicated	(Mt Horeb)	10 mths	11.5 mths	1/1/'2	Ex 40:17	Lev 1:1
12	Rules for Levites - Worship & Living	Mount Sinai					
13	First Census	Mount Sinai	4 weeks	12.5 mths	1/2/'2	Nu 1:1	
14	Second Passover	Mount Sinai			14/1/'2	Nu 9:1	
15	**Departed Sinai**	Mount Sinai	20 days	1 yr 1 mth	20/2/'2	Nu 10:11	
16	Complaint of Hardship - Fire & Quail	Kibroth				Nu 11:34	
17	Aaron & Miram Oppose Moses	Hazeroth				Nu 11:35	Nu 12:1
18	Journey to Canaan - Wilderness	Paran	11 days			Nu 12:16	De 1:19
19	**Spies Sent Out** - A Bad Report	Kadesh	40 days	1 yr 3 mths		Nu 13:1	Nu 14:1
20	Israel Driven Back - Entrance Denied	Hormah				Nu 14:45	De 1:45

#	Event	Location	Duration	Period	Date	Reference	Reference
21	**Wandering in Hill Country of Seir**	Seir	38 yrs				De 2:1
22	Death of Korah & 250 Leaders	Seir				Nu 16:1	
23	Aaron's Rod Budded - Leadership	Seir				Nu 17:1	
24	South to Ezion Gerber	Ezion Geber					Nu 33:35
25	Return to Kadesh - Miriam's Death	Kadesh	1 week			Nu 20:1	Nu 33:36
26	Water from the Rock - Meribar	Kadesh				Nu 20:8	
27	Moses Excluded From Entry	Kadesh				Nu 20:12	
28	Death of Aarom	Mt Hor	30 days	39 yr 3 mths	1/5/'40	Nu 20:24	Nu 33:38
29	Defeat of Arad, Canaanite King	Mt Hor				Nu 21:1	
30	Bronze Serpent - Impatience	Mt Hor				Nu 21:4	
31	Around Edom - Descendants of Esau	East Edom				Nu 21:4	De 2:8
32	Around Moab - Desendants of Lot	East Moab				Nu 21:11	De 2:9
33	South of Ammon - Descendants of Lot	Border				Nu 21:13	De 2:19
34	**Conquest of the Amorites**	East Jordan				Nu 21:31	De 3:12
35	Defeat of Sihon	Heshbon				Nu 21:21	De 2:24
36	Defeat of Og	Bashan				Nu 21:33	De 3:1
37	Moab Against Israel - Balak & Balaam	Plain of Moab				Nu 22:1	Nu 33:48
38	Israel Seduced - Immorality with Moab	Shittim				Nu 25:1	Nu 33:49
39	Second Census - the New Generation	Shittim					
40	Vengeance on Midian & Balaam	Shittim				Nu 31:1	
41	Joshua to Succeed Moses	Shittim				Nu 27:18	De 31:1
42	**Death of Moses**	Mount Nebo	30 days	39 yr 9.5 mth	1/11/'40		De 34:1
43	**Crossing Jordan**	Shittim				Jos 1:1	Jos 3:1
44	**Promised Land Entered**		40 years			Jos 4:1	

There are several ways of understanding the Bible Chronology –
Key Dates

Solomon was made king (this is the starting date[1])	970 BC	1Kin 2:12
Temple commenced in 4th year of Solomon's reign	966 BC	1Kin 6:1
Exodus occurred 480 years before Temple start	1446 BC	1Kin 6:1
God called Abraham 430 years before the Exodus	1876 BC	Gen 11:26
Abraham was born 75 years before the call	1951 BC	Gen 11:26
Flood to birth of Abraham was 292 years	2243 BC	
Adam to the Flood was 1656 years	3899 BC	
Abraham was born when Terah was age 70		
Abraham left Haran at 75 when Terah was 145		Gen 12:4
Terah died at 205, 60 years after Abraham left Haran		Gen 11:26
Abraham received the Promise at age 75		Gen 12:1
Jacob in Egypt 215 years after Abraham in Canaan		Acts 13:20
Israel was in Egypt 215 years		Gal 3:16,17

Differences with Ussher
1. Considers Terah was age 130 at the birth of Abraham - not 70 Gen 11:26. Abraham was in Haran till Terah died Acts 7:4 - (difference 60 years)
2. Considers the Divided Kingdom from Rehoboam to Zedekiah was 390 years duration (based on the addition of the number of years of each reign) - not 344 years (based on historical dates from 930 to 586 BC - (difference 46 years). This means the Temple was commenced 1012 AD - not 966 AD.

Other possible differences
3. Abraham received the Promise at 99 - not 75 (difference 24 years)
4. Israel was in Egypt 430 years Ex 12:40,43 - not 215 years (difference 215 years). Paul described the time from the giving of the promise to Abraham until the giving of the Law as 430 years Gal 3:16,17. The 430 years from the Promise to Abraham (at 75 years) to the Exile (ref p72). The 4th generation from Jacob to Moses allows 215 years Gen 15:16 (ref p74).

Legend
AM - Anno Mundi *year of the world - the appearance of Adam*
BC - *before Christ. - his birth is believed to be around 5 BC*
AD - Anno Domini *year of the Lord*
Ussher, James - Archbishop and Primate of Ireland 1581-1656 made a comprehensive assessment of the chronology recorded in the Old Testament - he calculated the date of the appearance of Adam as 4004 BC.
Other calculations of the Old Testament chronology include -
•   Johannes Kepler - 3992 BC
•   Sir Isaac Newton - 4000 BC
•   Jose ben Halafta - 3896 BC

---

[1]References - Westminister Encyclopedia p570; Illustrated Bible Dictionary p273

Old Testament Timeline Overview

	BC	years	years	Ussher BC	difference years
Adam	3899			4004	
Flood	2243	1656	1656	2348	
Abraham (birth)	1951		292	1996	60 *
Abraham (call)	1876	367	75	1921	
Family in Canaan			215		
Israel in Egpt	1661	430	215	1706	
Exodus	1446			1491	
Mt Sinai					
Wilderness			40		
Conquest	1406		5	1451	
Joshua (peace)			25		
Judges			326		
Eli					
Samuel					
United Kingdom			120		
Saul (reign)	1050			1095	
David (reign)	1010			1055	
Solomon (reign)	970			1015	
Temple Commmenced	966	480		1012	46 *
Divided Kingdom	930			975	
Exile of Judah	586		344	586	
Return	538	428	48	538	
		538	538		
Birth of Jesus	5			4	
totals		3899	3899		105
* Differences with Ussher					

Adam to Abraham Timeline

		years	AM		BC	AM	years	reference
Creation		1st son	died	age	3899			
Adam		130	930	930				Gen 5:3
Seth		105	1042	912				
Enosh		90	1140	905				
Kenan		70	1235	910				
Mahalalel		65	1290	895				
Jared		162	1422	962				
Enoch		65	987	365				
Methuselah		187	1656	969				
Lamech		182	1651	777				
		1056						
Noah	b				2843	1056		Gen 5:28
Year of the Flood				600	2243	1656	1656	Gen 8:13
The Flood occurred 1656 years after Adam								
After the Flood		1st son		age				
Shem		2		600				Gen 11:10
Aephanad		35		438				
Shelah		30		433				
Eber		34		464				
Peleg		30		239				
Reu		32		239				
Serug		30		230				
Nahor		29		148				
Terah		70		205				Gen 11:26
		292					292	
Flood to Abraham		292	Abraham was born 292 years after the Flood					
Abraham	b				1951	1948	75	Gen 11:26
called out				75	1876	2023		Gen 12:4
Abraham		25						Gen 21:5
Isaac		60						Gen 25:26
Jacob	?	80						Gen 41:46
Levi	?	61						
Kohath	?	62	In the 4th Generation					Gen 15:16
Amram	?	62	(Jacob to Moses)					
Moses	*	80	(215 years)					
		430	From the promise to the Law				430	Gal 3:17
Exodus					1446	2453		Ex 12:41
? Estimated			**Total years**				2453	
* Moses years to the Exodus								

Abraham to Temple Timeline

	Period	age	year	reference
Key Dates	Solomon was made king	19	970 BC	1Kin 2:10-12
	Temple commenced in 4th year of Solomon's reign	23	966 BC	1Kin 6:1
	Exodus occured 480 years before Solomon's 4th year		1446 BC	1Kin 6:1
	Abraham's promise until the Exodus was 430 years		1876 BC	Gal 3:17
Abraham	Abraham was born [1876 + 75]		1951 BC	Gen 11:26
	The promise to Abraham was received at age 75	75	1876 BC	Gen 12:1-4
	Abraham entered Canaan at age 75	75	1876 BC	Gen 12:1-4
	Isaac was born [1876-25]	100	1851 BC	Gen 21:5
	Abraham died [1951-175]	175	1776 BC	Gen 25:7
Isaac	Isaac was born 25 years later [1876-25]		1851 BC	Gen 21:5
	Jacob & Esau were born [1851-60]	60	1791 BC	Gen 25:24-26
	Isaac died [1851 - 180]	180	1671 BC	Gen 35:28
Jacob	Jacob was born [1851-60]		1791 BC	Gen 25:24-26
	Joseph was born [1791 - 91]	91	1700 BC	Gen 41:46
	Jacob entered Egypt [1791-130]	130	1661 BC	Gen 47:9
	Jacob died at age 147 [1791 - 147]	147	1644 BC	Gen 47:28
Joseph	Joseph was born [1661 + 30 +7 +2]		1700 BC	Gen 45:6
	Joseph became Prime Minister of Egypt	30	1670 BC	Gen 41:46
	Age when Jacob entered Egypt [30 + 7 + 2]	39	1661 BC	Gen 45:6
	Joseph died at age 110 [1700 - 110]	110	1590 BC	Gen 50:22
	Hykos rulers in Egypt 1700 - 1500 BC			
Moses	Moses was born 80 years before the Exodus		1526 BC	Ex 7:7
	Date of the Exodus [966 + 480]		1446 BC	Ex 12:40,41
	Moses died at age 120	120	1406 BC	Deut 34:7
Joshua	Joshua was born 40 years before the Exodus		1486 BC	Jos 14:7
	Israel entered the Promised Land [1446 - 40]	80	1406 BC	Jos 4:1; 5:6
	The Promised Land was settled under Joshua	85	1401 BC	Jos 14:10,11
	Joshua died at age 110 [1486 - 110]	110	1376 BC	Jos 24:29

Abraham to Exile Timeline

Period	years	year
Time from God's promise to Abraham to the Exodus		
Date of God's promise to Abraham at age 75		1876 BC
Birth of Isaac [1876 - 25]	25	1851 BC
Birth of Jacob [1851 - 60]	60	1791 BC
Entry of Jacob into Egypt [1791 - 130]	130	1661 BC
Duration of Abraham's family in Canaan	215	
Time until death of Joseph [110-39]	71	1590 BC
Time of the bondage of Israel in Egypt [1590 - 1446]	144	1446 BC
Duration of Israel in Egypt	215	
Duration of Abraham's descendents in Canaan & Egypt	430	
Period of the Judges		
Book of Judges - Death of Joshua to Eli [1376 - 1148]	228	
Period of Judges - Joshua to Saul [1376 - 1050]	326	
Period of the Kings		
United Kingdom	120	
Saul appointed king 1050 - 1010 BC		1050 BC
David appointed king 1010 - 970 BC		1010 BC
Solomon appointed king 970 - 930 BC		970 BC
Temple - commenced		966 BC
Divided Kingdom	344	
Solomon's son appointed king		930 BC
Israel conquered by Assyria - Dispersion		722 BC
Judah conquered by Babylon - Exile		586 BC
Return from Exile		538 BC
Theocracy		
From Mt Sinai to Saul [1446 - 1050]	396	
Monarchy		
From Saul to Exile [1050 - 586]	464	

Journey of Abraham into Promised Land

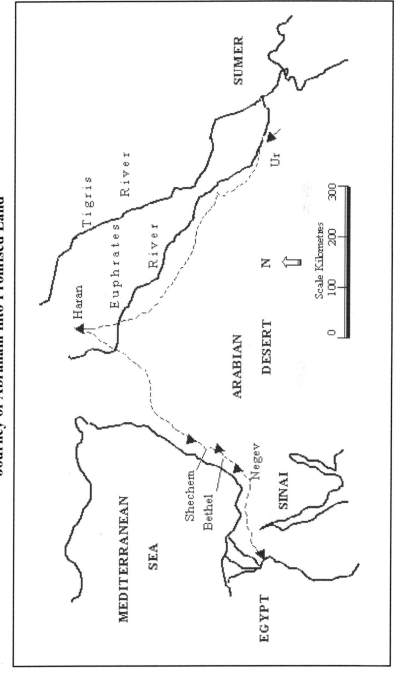

Deuteronomy

Chronology of the Old Testament

Periods	yrs		date BC	reign	age	yrs	description
BEGINNING		Adam	3899?				Cain, Abel, Seth
		b Noah	2843-1893		950		Flood 2243, Babel
PATRIACHS		b Abraham	1951-1776		175		Isaac, Jacob (ISRAEL)
		b Joseph	1700-1590		110		12 sons 12 Tribes
EXODUS		b Moses	1526-1406		120		Egypt, Mt Sinai, LAW
			1446 BC				1 Kings 6:1
CONQUEST		b Joshua	1486-1376		110		Promised Land
JUDGES		Judges	1375-1148	257	225		Gideon, Sampson
		Eli	1148-1080	68	98		incl sons
		Samuel	1080-1050	55	85		overlap with Saul
KINGDOM UNITED		Saul	1050-1010	40	70		First king
		David	1010-970	40	70		Nathan
Jerusalem		Solomon	970-930	40	59		Temple - 966 to 959

JUDAH

	yrs	Kings	reign BC
KINGDOM DIVIDED			
South	17	Rehoboam	930-914
Jerusalem	3	Abijah	913-911
344 years	41	Asa *	910-870
(930 - 586)			
* 8 kings were good			
12 knigs were evil			
Prophets			
	25	Jehoshaphat *	873-849

ISRAEL

Kings	reign BC	yrs	description
			North
Jeroboam 1	930-910	22	Samaria
Nadab	910-909	2	208 years
Bassha	909-886	24	(930 - 722)
Elah	886-885	2	9 kings were evil
Zimri	885		
Omri	885-874	12	**Prophets**
Ahab	874-853	22	Elijah 874-852 22
Ahaziah	853-852	2	Elisha 852-798 54

Prophets (Judah)			Kings of Judah	Date	Yrs	Kings of Israel	Date	Yrs	Prophets (Israel)		
			Jehoram	849-842	8	Joram	852-841	12			
			Ahaziah	841		Jehu	841-814	28			
			Athaliah	841-836	6						
			Joash	* 836-797	40						
						Jehoahaz	814-798	17			
			Amaziah	* 797-768	29	Jehoash	798-782	16	Jonah	760	
			Azariah	* 791-740	52	Jeroboam II	793-753	41	Amos	760-750	10
			(Uzziah)			Zechariah	753-752		Hosea	757-722	35
						Shallum	752				
Isaiah	740-690	50	Jotham	* 751-736	16	Menahem	751-742	10			
						Pekahiah	741-740	2			
Micah	740-700	40	Ahaz	736-721	16	Pekah	740-732	20			
			Hezekiah	* 721-693	29	Hosea	731-722	9			
Nahum	622-612	10	Manasseh	693-639	55	**Fall of Israel 722**		155			
Zephaniah	625		Amon	639		(Samaria)					
Jeremiah	626-580	46	Josiah	* 639-609	31						
Joel	600		Jehoahaz	609		Fall of Assyria	612				
Habakkuk	600		Jehoiakim	608-598	11	(Nineveh)					
Obadiah	586		Jehoiachin	598							
Daniel	590-533	57	Zedekiah	597-586	11						
Ezekiel	593-571	22	**Fall of Judah 586**		304						
			(Jerusalem)								
			First captives	605							
CAPTIVITY			Fall of Babylon	539		After 70 years	605-538				
RETURN			First return	538		Temple dedicated	516				
Haggai	520-516	4	Esther	480							
Zechariah	520-516	4	Ezra	458-430	28						
Malachi	430		Nehemiah	445-430	15						
SILENT YEARS				400-0							

Birth of the **LORD JESUS CHRIST**

BOOKS OF THE BIBLE
[39 + 27 = 66]

BOOKS OF THE OLD TESTAMENT
[39]

	HISTORY (17)	POETRY (5)	PROPHECY (17)	
LAW (5)	Genesis	Job	Isaiah	**MAJOR (5)**
Pentateuch	Exodus	Psalms	Jeremiah	
Books of Moses	Leviticus	Proverbs	Lamentations	
	Numbers	Ecclesiastes	Ezekiel	
	Deuteronomy	Solomon	Daniel	
HISTORY (12)	Joshua		Hosea	**MINOR (12)**
of Israel	Judges		Joel	
	Ruth		Amos	
	1 Samuel		Obadiah	
	2 Samuel		Jonah	
	1 Kings		Micah	
	2 Kings		Nahum	
	1 Chronicles		Habakkuk	
	2 Chronicles		Zephaniah	
	Ezra	Post Exile	Haggai	
	Nehemiah		Zechariah	
	Esther		Malachi	

BOOKS OF THE NEW TESTAMENT
[27]

	HISTORY (5)	LETTERS OF PAUL (13)	GENERAL LETTERS (9)	
GOSPELS (4)	Matthew	Romans	Hebrews	Unknown
	Mark	1 Corinthians	James	Other
	Luke	2 Corinthians	1 Peter	Apostles (7)
	John	Glatians	2 Peter	
Early Church (1)	Acts	Ephesians	1 John	
Luke		Philippians	2 John	
		Colossians	3 John	
		1 Thessalonians	Jude	
		2 Thessalonians	Revelation	John
		1 Timothy		
		2 Timothy		
		Titus		
		Philemon		

The Layman's Commentary Series contains the following –

Volume 1 – Book of the Law Volume 2 – Books of History Volume 3 – Books
      of Wisdom
Volume 4 – Books of the Prophets
Volume 5 – Books of the Gospels
Volume 6 – Acts of the Apostles
Volume 7 – Epistles of Paul
Volume 8 – General Epistles

The Series contains the following features -
Facts, figures & dates, tables & cross referencing
Some 600 pages in total
Background information
Chronologies of the Bible, Kings, Prophets, Acts
of the Early Church
Harmony of the Gospels
Miracles & healings of Jesus
Prophecies concerning Jesus
Chronology & tabulation of Revelation
Leadership principles of Jesus, Joseph, Joshua, David,
Nehemiah, Mordecia, Xerxes, Esther